Intimacy and Type

Intimacy and Type

A Practical Guide
for Improving Relationships
for Couples and Counselors

Jane Hardy Jones, Ed.D.
Ruth G. Sherman, Ph.D.

Center for Applications of Psychological Type, Inc.
Gainesville, Florida

Published by
Center for Applications of Psychological Type, Inc.
2815 N.W. 13th Street, Suite 401
Gainesville, FL 32609
(352) 375-0160 • (800) 777-2278

CAPT, the CAPT logo, and Center for Applications of Psychological Type are
trademarks of Center for Applications of Psychological Type, Inc., Gainesville, FL.

Myers-Briggs Type Indicator and MBTI are registered trademarks of
Consulting Psychologists Press, Inc., Palo Alto, CA.

Printed in the United States of America.

ISBN 0-935652-23-X

Library of Congress Cataloging-in-Publication Data
Jones, Jane Hardy, 1927–
Intimacy and type : a practical guide for improving relationships
for couples and counselors / Jane Hardy Jones, Ruth G. Sherman.
p. cm.
Includes bibliographical references.
ISBN 0-935652-23-X
1. Typology (Psychology) 2. Myers-Briggs Type Indicator.
3. Interpersonal relations. 4. Interpersonal conflict. 5. Intimacy
(Psychology) 6. Love. I. Sherman, Ruth G., 1921–1996. II. Title.
BF698.3.J66   1997
158.2—dc21   97-20795
                                    CIP

To Isabel Briggs Myers . . .

Who dreamed and worked to
help people by the application
of Jung's typology to the
understanding and appreciation
of differences.

Do not try to change me or criticize me; mirror me to myself so I can see *me* and choose to grow in my own ways.

Love me as I am, different from you. Value my differences and let them be strengths between us so we can rely on each other and grow with each other.

When I see your dark side, if I am angry or frightened by it, I will ask you to take responsibility for it, but I will not blame you or ask you to apologize. If you see me standing in my shadow, bring in the light gently, please, or call me on it matter-of-factly, but do not blame me or ask me to apologize.

Let's not have a you and me relationship only, let's have an *us* relationship, too!

Contents

Contents

Contents

Contents

Foreword

We are two psychologists who have each spent more than twenty-five years doing pre-marital, marital, and post-marital counseling at the University of Hawaii and in private practice. We have also done relationship counseling with unmarried, gay, lesbian, committed and uncommitted couples. During that time we have seen literally thousands of couples experiencing difficulties or conflicts in some aspect of their relationships.

Almost without exception, we have used an instrument called the Myers-Briggs Type Indicator (MBTI) in working with these couples. And almost without exception, we have found this instrument useful.

We have trained our staff and interns at the Counseling Center in the use of the MBTI for faculty and community groups. The Indicator is now the most widely used of the psychological measures given on the U.H. campus.

In the late '70s, Ruth used the MBTI in an extensive research project using 167 couples to identify the effect of type on satisfaction in marriage. For this piece of research, Ruth was awarded the first Isabel Briggs-Myers Memorial Fund Award for Research.

Jane was one of the earliest users of the MBTI, beginning in 1965 when she was a doctoral student at Auburn University. W. Harold Grant, Director of Auburn's Counseling Center, gave the MBTI to his tests and measurements class. Jane responded very positively to the instrument, studied the first MBTI *Manual* (1962) and, upon graduation, brought the MBTI to Hawaii where she introduced it to Ruth. Together, they began to use more answer sheets than anyone else in the country. Myers asked to meet with them at an American Psychological Association convention since they were so clearly delighted with her work. Thus began a long and wonderful affiliation with one of the test creators. Isabel Myers was indeed a very special person and truly dedicated to her work.

The MBTI is an instrument based on the theory developed by Carl Gustav Jung and explained in his book, *Psychological Types*. Many of you are probably familiar with Jung and some of his theories. It is advantageous, but not necessary, to understand his theories in order to be able to understand the MBTI and this book.

Katharine Cook Briggs and her daughter, Isabel Briggs Myers, devoted much of their lives to the study of Jung's theories and development of their instrument. Myers' son, Peter Myers, and former daughter-in-law Kathy Myers, are still deeply involved in the work Katharine Briggs and Isabel Myers began. Many others, especially Mary McCaulley of the Center for Applications of Psychological Type (CAPT) in Gainesville, Florida, have spent years assisting others in applying and researching theories related to type for the constructive use of differences.

The couples with whom we have worked have indicated that they knew themselves better, understood their partner more fully, and were able to understand why their conflicts were occurring as a result of understanding their MBTI results. Understanding is just the first step in resolving those conflicts, of course, but it does provide the necessary base for moving ahead to deal effectively with the differences and misunderstandings.

The first part of this book is devoted to basic Myers-Briggs Type Indicator and Jungian concepts of psychological type. There are four basic preferences for functioning in the world which combine in 16 different ways. These preferences relate to how we perceive the world and ourselves and how we make decisions.

The descriptions of the preferences in Chapter I are, for the most part, about primary preferences for functioning. That is, they are descriptions of the mental functions at their purest, when they are the favorite function.

Also included in the first part of the book are descriptions of how individuals of each of the 16 types would typically or usually, but not always behave. The unconscious can have quite an impact on our behavior. The behaviors we are discussing for the most part are the individual's *conscious* orientation to life and the world.

We speak to individuals and to couples in this book. Marriage counselors may want to recommend the book to couples or use it as a conceptual framework in their own counseling. The observations and suggestions we make come from our work with couples supplemented by research on the Myers

Briggs Type Indicator and relationship satisfaction data from couples who had been in the relationship for 2 years or more.

Because we have found this instrument and the knowledge it brings so useful in our practice, we want to offer the understanding and concepts it brings to as wide a range of individuals as possible. In addition to our regular counseling, we have done large workshops for imparting this information, but we were still not satisfied that we were reaching a large enough audience with information that could improve their relationships.

We would like to take special notice of Mary McCaulley and Charles Martin, as well as others at CAPT for carefully going over the text and providing insightful comments. Leslie Kathleen Jones (Jane's daughter) also made valuable contributions to the final product. With careful input from them and many others, the results are markedly enhanced. Our thanks go to the many people, especially our clients and patients who contributed so much to our knowledge. The counseling sessions and individuals described in this book have been modified to protect the people involved and names have been changed as well. The basic dynamics are faithfully presented.

Note: Though it is not grammatically accurate, we have chosen to use "they" and "their" in this book even when the antecedent is singular. We have done this to avoid using both "she" and "he" or alternating he and she. We hope it is less distracting from the text.

CHAPTER I

Preferences in Life and Love

"In spite of all indignant protests to the contrary, the fact remains that love, its problems and its conflicts, is of fundamental importance in human life and, as careful inquiry consistently shows, is of far greater significance than the individual suspects."
—C. G. Jung

A Preference for Difference

You are different. It is a gift to be unique. Yet there are personal styles that can be characterized in general to aid our understanding of our relationships. If we gain enough perspective we may even be able to laugh at things about ourselves and others that made us upset or angry before. Carl Jung, Katharine Briggs, and Isabel Myers have given us a way to get perspective on ourselves. They have described natural differences between people in the ways they orient themselves to the world, the ways they prefer to take in information, and how they arrive at decisions. Understanding these natural preferences increases our choices and provides us maximum freedom.

If you want a simple way to understand what we mean when we use the word "preference," think in terms of your two hands. If you're right-handed, that is your *preferred* hand. It doesn't mean you don't use your left hand—everyone does every day. Try this exercise: On a blank piece of paper write your name using your preferred hand. Then write your name using your other hand. Unless you're very different from most of us, the first time you wrote your name you were more comfortable than the second, and the product was also better.

Please keep this example in mind as we discuss your "preferences," because while one style is what you will use most often and be most comfortable with, you will also remember examples of when you demonstrated the opposite or a different type of behavior.

If we are light and playful sometimes in this book, just play and enjoy along with us. But also look deeper, beyond the laughter, and hear a message that could change your life—if you'll allow it. We do not want to minimize your uniqueness by classifying or pigeonholing you with these general descriptions. On the contrary, we honor our own individuality and yours. We just want you to have a model for better understanding yourself and others.

Understanding another style *does not* mean putting up with behaviors that are destructive to you. It means being clear about what you are like and what your partner is like and what you can reasonably expect in a relationship. It does not mean you (or your partner) have permission to act in the worst ways your mother or father acted or to recreate conflicts from the past. Carl Jung asks that we become more conscious, and through this become aware of having more choices. In having more choices, we become more free.

The bottom line is you can always leave a relationship; but you can also choose to stay and deal with some of the very qualities that attracted you in the beginning and which may now have a negative side. You can deal with your own negative behavior that an intimate relationship inevitably triggers.

Many people don't mind working at work, but don't think they should have to work on a relationship. We believe a good relationship with another human being is the most essential ingredient for a satisfying life. This means it is well worth the time and effort to see the relationship realistically and to make choices and take actions that enhance the relationship. This usually demands that you grow as a person in the process. Sometimes an outside perspective may be necessary to help both of you see the forces between you and to help you move toward a more rewarding relationship; but much can also be done without an outside view if you increase your own awareness and insight. Especially if both people are well motivated, it need not take a very long time. If you want to do it on your own, this book is designed to help you understand where you and your partner are now and get you to where you want to be—we hope with some laughter along the way.

Needed: A Model for Equality Without Sameness

It is a major challenge to have a relationship with an equal partner. In spite of the emergence of more and more writers offering descriptions of how equal partners might relate, in many homes it is often still assumed the father is the "head" of the household. Even in homes where an equal partnership is sought, negative reactions can still arise as fantasies or stereotypes of the perfect relationship are not fulfilled. More clarity may be needed about expectations of self and others before entering a partnership.

We need to meet the challenge and create a model or models flexible enough to fit any couple, yet structured enough so that every decision doesn't have to be debated and discussed at length. Where do we turn for a model of equality without sameness?

As you grow up Mom and/or Dad are older and "in charge." Your brother or sister, if you have one, is younger or older. Your boss at work is designated to have some power over you. Mom and Dad may understand role differences better than how to be equal. They may not have even addressed the issue. Maybe they just did the best they could given their experience and state of collective consciousness of the time into which they were born.

Business partnerships often reflect an equal relationship, but such partnerships do not always work well. Friendship is really the only arena in which we can find an equal. Friendship is, however, different from an intimate sexual relationship. The intensity that develops in an intimate relationship is not usually present at the same level in a friendship. It is easier to say no to a friend than a partner. It is easier to walk away and come back later or never come back. There is more freedom and there is more choice. Friendship, therefore, may not provide the perfect model for an equal partnership, but it is a place to start.

What if we said never treat your partner worse than your best friend? Is that a criterion you would want included? What other parameters might be discussed and adopted or rejected? How do you make decisions if someone doesn't have veto power?

We will not pretend to answer these questions for you. At this point, each individual couple needs to struggle with their own solutions. In the process new "truths" of our time will hopefully evolve to clarify our intimate relationships.

Relating as equals takes some consciousness. Two independent people may find the compromises or negotiations required are too high a price to pay. Two dependent people may have difficulty leaving even if they want to. One independent and one dependent person need to be clear what each is contributing to the relationship to avoid unequal input. If one is dependent emotionally and one financially, is that O.K?

It is not easy to allow yourself and another—especially your mate, partner, or lover—to be different. Seeing the similarities or differences positively enhances the relationship. We will help you find ways to use differences and similarities constructively for a better marriage or relationship. Don't try to change your partner to be like yourself. Appreciate yourself *and* be glad there is so much variety from which to choose your mate.

Before we go into detailed descriptions of the functions of the Myers-Briggs Type Indicator (MBTI), here are two examples of how we use the Indicator with couples. They may help you understand why we find the MBTI so valuable.

Most people have more problems when there are differences, so we'll use examples in which difference has been a problem.

A Tale of Two Couples

Thinking Man/Feeling Woman

One couple we worked with were David and Betty. Both were in their sixties. They had been married over 40 years and had three grown children. They are Caucasian, Catholic, and had grown up on the East Coast. They were referred by a church counselor who felt she was not being effective in working with them.

As reported by her first counselor, Betty would spend almost the entire session crying. David would spend the session being defensive. There had never been any major problems between them such as drugs, alcohol, infidelity, or gambling. They both considered themselves moral, ethical people. Betty had reached a point where she was considering either divorce or suicide as an alternative to continuing a situation in which she was so desperately unhappy.

At our second session, we asked them to take the Myers-Briggs Type Indicator to help them look at their marriage from a wider perspective. Both

Betty and David are introverts (if you are not familiar with the terms extravert or introvert, you will become so as you read the book). Both Betty and David also prefer to deal with practical reality and factual data; the information they prefer to handle is perceived through their five senses. They also like their outer world—their environment—to be organized.

The primary difference between the partners in this couple was that David made his decisions with his head believing that if there were a "logical" reason for doing something that was the thing to do. Betty, on the other hand, listened to her heart, and people's feelings were of primary importance in reaching a decision.

Strange as it may appear, they had never been aware of the difference between them. Slowly, and with much coaching, David was able to stop defending his position as past issues arose in our sessions. Also with much coaching, Betty learned how to present her experiences in the marriage without blaming or attacking.

All of her life, Betty had tried to be a "good" daughter, wife and mother. This had meant doing what was expected of her and not expressing her own needs. Finally, the resentments had grown so great, she was no longer able to control her emotions. David came to therapy hoping Betty could be "fixed."

It took about three months before Betty and David could listen to each other and learn to laugh at themselves and each other. At that point, they were communicating more effectively and really enjoying being with each other. He needed her warmth and feeling responsiveness when she could use them positively. She needed his logical thinking when he wasn't using it to criticize her. They both reported that the "test" had contributed to their understanding and acceptance of their differences.

Extraverted Woman/Introverted Man

Sally and Frank were a couple who also reported the MBTI was helpful in improving their relationship. Sally, an outgoing Caucasian with strong feelings, had met Frank, a quiet, sensitive Japanese man, in graduate school on the East Coast. Despite parental objections, they married and mutually agreed to move to Hawaii where mixed ethnic marriages are more common and more acceptable. They had two children, ages 4 and 6, who were healthy and active.

Overall both Sally and Frank reported their marriage as satisfactory, but wanted help to understand the differences in their needs, and skills to resolve their conflicts.

Frank worked in human resource development for a large corporation; he had constant and intense interactions with the individuals he supervised. Sally had decided to put her career on the shelf and to devote her time and energy to her family. She was slowly growing resentful because she had become dependent on Frank for adult interaction. The greater her need became the more it appeared to her that he withdrew and withheld. Frank, on the other hand, stated that he was a faithful, hard-working husband and Sally was becoming unreasonable in her demands.

In therapy we looked at the differences between extraverts (Sally) and introverts (Frank). Sally learned it was unrealistic to expect Frank to make up for her lack of interaction with others. Frank learned that it was all right for Sally to need more communication with him than he did with her. They each assumed responsibility for improving the situation. Sally joined the League of Women Voters where she found several rewarding friendships. She also felt she was back in her adult world.

Frank discovered that working in his garden replenished and renewed his energy. So as soon as he came home he changed his clothes and gave himself an hour in the yard by himself. Then he felt like going in and sharing his day with Sally.

Both Sally and Frank became less blaming and more understanding of each other's needs. It is very useful to know that some of your partner's behavior which may annoy you is usually an expression of natural style and not a deliberate choice to be difficult. We always ask both people to work on the things that are getting in the way of the relationship working. It is almost never only one person who needs to change and become more conscious. If no one is to "blame," we can move farther, faster in resolving the issues.

The Preferences

The MBTI describes the preferences of people on four dimensions: extraversion/introversion, sensing/intuition, thinking/feeling, and judging/perceiving. For each of these, we will describe typical behaviors and attitudes developed by people with this preference. You will probably be able to identify most of your partner's and your own preferences. Remember: the goal is to value the differences and use them positively. If you are right-handed, it will be like identifying the way you use your right hand best. The four words or letters not chosen indicate what your left hand (or unconscious) has to offer when you can tap into it, usually later in life. The best way to know your type is to take the Myers-Briggs Type Indicator. It is available from a wide range of psychologists, counselors, and other consultants. In the meantime, you can use your best estimate based on our descriptions.

Extraversion and Introversion

DIRECTION OF ENERGY

Some people rush out to meet life; others peek at it from around the corner before deciding whether to come out and be seen. These are broad generalizations and they apply more to some people than others. In children (before they develop their masks of social behavior), these behaviors can be quite pronounced. One child may rush up while you're eating your ice cream cone and demand, "I want a bite"; while another may look at you, shyly smile, and hope that you'll offer some.

In America we tend to value outgoing people: we seem to think it is healthier to ask for what you want. We try to train the quiet boy to behave the same as the outgoing one, while still saying we value individuality.

Carl Jung, on the other hand, saw both ways as valuable. He called the outgoing energy "extraverting" and the ingoing energy "introverting". The MBTI uses E for extraverting and I for introverting; the following diagram shows the direction of energy flow.

$$\boxed{\leftarrow\leftarrow\leftarrow \text{I} \mid \text{E} \rightarrow\rightarrow\rightarrow}$$

Now, let's get more specific—extraverting sets up a different style of interacting with others than does introverting. These differences are described below.

For Types Who Extravert (E)

You are outgoing and want contact—physical contact, mental contact, emotional contact. You don't want to be out there by yourself if you can help it. You get energized by talking, working, and playing with a wide variety of people. You can get bored easily if there's not a lot going on. You are stimulated by a lot of talking and activity. You notice people's body language, but you prefer to be told rather than assume you know what it means. You can get very angry, but once the anger is out you usually get over it quickly. You are at ease with the environment, and like to be active. You like variety, excitement, and stimulation from the outside. You talk easily and like feedback from others. Talking it out or getting other people's opinions helps you decide what you think of, or feel about, a situation. Sometimes you make statements just to see what effect they will have on others. You interact a lot with the environment, so that any feelings or thoughts you pick up, positive or negative, are likely to be included in our conversations with other people. Since your behavior is highly interactive, you tend to take in what you need and then move on. You would say you don't hold a grudge. At a party you are usually a good mixer and like to be included. You can be a big help with long silences. You tend to look for explanations of problems in the people and events around you. At your worst, you won't stop talking, interrupt others, and insist on "having it out," even following the other person who may be trying to get away. At your best, you're a fun and energizing companion, aware of what's going on in the world and able to be a part of it.

For Types Who Introvert (I)

You are quiet. You're reflective. You take time to answer and make up your mind. You are slow to anger, but sometimes slow in getting over anger. You want deep meaningful conversation with a few people you consider very special or maybe just one at a time. Your privacy is important. You regenerate your energy when you are alone. You don't like a noisy environment. When you have to make a lot of new contacts in a single day, you are tired and need quiet to regenerate.

On the other hand, when you are propelled by some deeper meaning, you can seem tireless. You are cautious with the environment. You may appear to others to be shy, reserved, or inscrutable. You are generally wary of new contacts and don't like to go to parties where you don't know anyone. If you do find someone you know or enjoy, you tend to get into long intense conversations rather than mingling with the whole group. Your apparent stubbornness is your way of not being manipulated by the environment since you don't want to have to "fight for your rights." However, you will stand firm if something precious is threatened, often to the surprise of the other person. You may tend to look for explanations of problems in your own actions and feelings. At your worst, you withdraw into your private world and refuse to come out, maybe for hours or days, sometimes refusing to say what is bothering you. At your best you are an attentive listener, who provides a safe harbor from the difficulties of the outer world and a different perspective on it.

Now decide which is your preference: E or I.

Sensing and Intuition

Some people prefer to experience their present reality and others prefer to imagine the possibilities. We all do some of both, even if we have a preference for one. We are each a little better with one than the other. The people who prefer to deal with the "real" world we call sensing types; the people who prefer to deal with the world they can imagine we call intuitive types. It was Jung's idea to do it this way to help separate the "sensible ones" from the "imaginative ones." It has to do with how you get your information—whether primarily through your five senses or your intuitive hunches. Both sensing and intuition are designated irrational functions since they are not based on or derived from reasoning. The information is just there to be perceived.

For Sensing Types (S)

You like the facts. You like to have information that can be seen, heard, touched, smelled, tasted. You want data to back up the theory. You are realistic, factual, concrete, detailed. You deal with *sense* instead of what one sensing type called the *"non"-sense* of the intuitive. You prefer the straightforward rather than the complex. You focus on the here and now and not what might be. You are a doer,—what good is an idea if it cannot be made into a reality? You like nature, smells, textures, spices, pleasant sounds, things that are *real*. You are fun loving and enjoy sports and nature. Your spirituality is likely to be experienced in the environment, when you are out communing with nature. You tend to be good with your hands and like a tangible product from your labor. Theories and abstractions do not interest you.

At your worst you think the way it has been is the way it always will be; any possibilities you think of will only make things worse. It is hard to listen to people who ask you to look at the situation another way. At your best you are competent at identifying tangible problems and you are usually able to know what to do about them.

For Intuitive Types (N)*

Intuition is *knowing*. You don't believe or think, you *know*. You are quick to see the patterns in details, without the careful examination of details one at a time. You dislike details, but love to dream up things. You love to explore the possibilities, to play in the beyond, to fly in to the air psychologically and pretend you don't have to come down. You like complexity and may create it where you don't find it. You like abstraction and prefer an abstract that cuts across the board rather than dealing with a multitude of details. You just don't want to "clutter up" your mind with all those bits of information. If your intuition is tuned on the outer world you may wish to be all things to all people, the Renaissance person. Or, you may direct your intuition into creating systems, making paradigms, seeing patterns. If it is directed on the inner world, your intuition may give you a vision of how things could be if only your own behavior and others' behavior would accommodate that vision. Your spirituality is likely to come from being in touch with the infinite, with something that transcends time and space. Whether you turn intuition to the outer or inner world, intuition is useful for transitions and creative process.

At your worst you ignore the facts, dream the dream, and spin off into a fanciful space which can appear weird, or far-out, resistant to coming back and coping with reality. At your best, you have a quick insight into the options available, and what the results of each option would be. When you have a hunch or imagine something, you can "see" it. You don't reason it out logically. It is just there. You see it so clearly you just know it is right.

Now decide which is your preference: S or N.

*The MBTI uses <u>N</u> instead of I so that <u>in</u>tuition is not confused with <u>i</u>ntroversion.

Thinking and Feeling

DECISION-MAKING MODE

Some people prefer to think about things and others prefer to feel about them. You might say this is your way of processing the information you get from your senses or your insights. If you're making a decision, is your head or your heart more important? Do you want to be reasonable or responsive? It's nice to be able to be both, but when you have to choose, which way does it go? Both thinking and feeling are rational processes based on the information obtained either through the senses or intuition. There is an information-based process behind the decisions made or conclusions drawn.

For Thinking Types (T)

You can be analytical, conceptual, discriminative, or integrative—pulling the concepts together. When thinking is active and directed, you seek to understand the things you have perceived with your sensing or intuition. You are somewhat detached from the person or thing that is being analyzed in order to get more perspective and see more angles. You want to figure "it" out—to know why someone or something does what they do. At the very least, you want to know—what does it mean? You allow for alternatives and choices. You look for the logic of things, and you may enjoy developing systems and principles to explain things. You can tie the past, present, and future together, and you can describe how one thing logically leads to the next. You love a good argument and may even engage in verbal debates or competition for the fun of it. You are better at trouble-shooting than at harmony-making. At your worst you are cool, critical, detached (sometimes *hot* and critical). At your best, you exemplify and embody knowledge, and you may be an expert in strategy and tactics, with a gift for figuring out what the next move should be to get the results that are sought.

For Feeling Types (F)

You embrace the world, preferring to "touch" the things you care about and which you have perceived with your senses or your intuition. The people you respond to positively can be warmed just by being in your presence. The feeling function, like thinking, is also a rational process. Feeling makes decisions based on the *values* held by the individual, what they consider to be *important* in life: what they care about. (Emotional responses are in a different category from feeling decision-making, which is a rational process. Emotional responses are not discussed here.) Some values are deeply based in internal or external experience and are difficult to change, while others seem more fluid as you change your estimate of the values at stake in this moment. A desire for harmony and concern for others, however, is often an ongoing value for feeling types. A thought can be captured in words fairly easily. Words about a feeling are often less exact translations of the experience. The feeling function, like the thinking function, can also be used to play interpersonal "games"*, but its purpose is not to engage the other in an analytical contest and demand logic, but to have an impact on the other— positive or negative. Neither "game" is always conscious in the person playing. At your worst you are over-sensitive, reactive, intense, and stuck in a bad evaluation of the situation. At your best your love and concern for others shines from your eyes and others experience your caring.

Now decide which is your preference: T or F.

* We call it a "game" if there is some implicit, unexplained, perhaps even unacknowledged demand that the other person respond in a certain way (i.e., in your style) in the verbal or non-verbal exchange. There may be a possible punitive aspect of being judged negatively or a feeling of being "put down" if the other person does not respond in the expected way.

Judging and Perceiving
RESPONSE TO ENVIRONMENT

Some people see the world as an open free space; others look for the underlying structures. These preferences make a difference in the way you respond to people and situations. If you hate to give up your options, the openness is appealing. If you like to know where you stand, the structures lend support. In any case, they are your way of responding to your environment.

If You Prefer a Judging Style (J)

You like structure, and you find it supports you. If you organize, set priorities, and decide, the world somehow has less control of you. There is security in structure—even if you change it tomorrow.

You are selective. You organize information in manageable ways. You make categories and decisions. You are responsible. You can move fast and decide, but are not necessarily "caught" in your decisions. You can often re-decide just as quickly. You evaluate an object as soon as it is perceived, so that the two step process seems like one. This means you automatically come to some assessment of whatever you are dealing with; sometimes prematurely, of course. It is difficult for you to separate your perception of the object from your assessment of it. The object must be reprocessed to change the assessment or to be open to a new view of things. You may perceive this as a waste of time since you can be impatient. You can get anxious if you have to keep things open and undecided. At your worst you can tediously repeat "the rule" and not understand why the other person doesn't see how important it is—like an overly responsible parent full of "shoulds"—even controlling. At your best, you can get an amazing amount of work done by your ability to plan, organize, and put first things first whether they are pleasant tasks or not.

If You Prefer a Perceiving Style (P)

Your world is full if interesting things. You are free-flowing and open. Since something new may turn up you don't want to make decisions until there is a need to do so. There is excitement variety and in exploring new routes. Decisions can be hard because they eliminate interesting choices. You are often clearer about what you *don't* want than what you *do* want. You prefer to be available for lots of other options that sound interesting. Perception is receptive. You are open to all the new information you can find and the things you can discover. It is like a quest without a pre-determined goal—to be aware and to process, but not necessarily evaluate the discovery or the process. Judging helps with bringing to closure; perceiving helps with exploring. At your worst you can be insecure, indecisive, and resistant—a rebellious "kid" slipping out of responsibility, even to yourself. At your best you are a curious discoverer of the world's secrets and knowledge, without necessarily having to do something about your discoveries, except perhaps to share them.

Now decide which is your preference: J or P.

If you put all four letters together, you have your type pattern, e.g. ESTJ, INFP, etc. It is best to validate your type preferences by actually taking the MBTI. For those who have not yet taken the Indicator, what would you say are your four letters?

E or I	S or N	T or F	J or P

Potential Positive/Negative Aspects of Each Preference

Each preference is valuable and has its own particular strengths. Each also has some characteristic weaknesses or pitfalls. The following chart can help you see both sides of each preference.

Positive		Negative	
E	I	E	I
Speak up	Listen attentively	Press the point	Concede the point
Initiate	Respond	Argue	Avoid argument
Socialize	Protect privacy	Intimidate	Retreat
Be active	Be reflective	Blame	Not respond
Energize	Calm	Be "outer" absorbed	Be "self" absorbed
S	N	S	N
Do	Know	Be nitty gritty	Be off the wall
Have a method	Have an idea	Oversimplify	Overcomplicate
Be factual	Be imaginative	Tack to the wall	Fly off
Have hands on	Have a hunch	Ignore the creative	Ignore the facts
Practical solutions	Imaginative solutions	Tinker	Day dream
T	F	T	F
Analyze	Care	Criticize	Smother
Devise	Value	Demand reasons	Demand values
Be fair	Be responsive	Out strategize	Out emotionalize
Keep cool	Show warmth	Be icy	Be gushy
Be objective	Be personal	Be patronizing	Be contemptuous
J	P	J	P
Be organized	Be spontaneous	Be a clockwatcher	Be late
Plan fun times	Be fun	Be closeminded	Lose direction
Be on time	Be flexible	Be authoritarian	Be undependable
Be decisive	Be open	Have a lot of "shoulds"	Be disorganized
Hang tough	Hang loose	Lecture	Space out

Interactions of Opposites

You may have a preference not only for the kind of partner you want, but also for the kind of communication or interaction you want at home. Or, more likely you will choose the person you can relate to best and who meets your other requirements for a mate and you just hope the dynamics at home will live up to expectations. Here are some ideas of what to expect if you and your partner are different on a preference dimension. If you are the same, other problems can arise which we will talk about later.

Interactions Between Extraverts and Introverts

Extraverts tend to "come forward" and introverts tend to "withdraw." The more traumatic the circumstances or the discussion, the more pronounced the behavior. That is, if extraverts are in a tight spot emotionally, they tend to want to confront and work it out or at least get rid of their feelings. Introverts, on the other hand, hate to "hassle" or fight and will go out of their way to avoid a fight or confrontation. Because introverts receive energy more than they put out energy, intense negative energy coming in their direction affects them more deeply. They may even make concessions they later wish they hadn't. This may be especially true when introversion is combined with a preference for feeling. Extraverts have a natural barrier since they are always ready with a comeback. They tend to stay involved regardless of the discussion content. Extraverts gain energy from interacting with others; introverts gain energy through time alone.

So, if extraverts want to talk about things and introverts want to be alone, especially if things get intense, what do they do if they're in a relationship together? Or what do you do if you're in a relationship with someone with different needs than yours? In a research study of couples by one of the authors, introverted men tend to marry extraverted women, but have trouble later with the interaction style. Remember though that extraverts do have an introverted side, like a "non-dominant hand" or less-used side, just as introverts have an extraverted side.

EXAMPLE: EXTRAVERTS WITH INTROVERTS

In the couples we see introverted men are often attracted to and may marry extraverted women. The men like the outgoing, social, vivacious style of the extraverted woman. It is unfortunately true that the very things that attract and are strengths can also be a problem. A couple like this fits the stereotype to some extent of the woman who wants to talk a lot and the man who wants her to be quiet. Extraverted women with introverted men do express some common difficulties: "He won't talk to me." "I don't know what he's thinking." "He won't let me in."

Regardless of gender, introverts want and need more time alone and more quiet. Extraverts need and want more interaction and action. If the difference in attitude or orientation to the outer world can be used to handle different necessities of life rather than to be annoyed with each other, apparent problems can be turned into benefits. The introvert may be more adept at what the extravert would consider a lonely task such as writing letters or doing research. The extravert may be more able and willing to handle people and situations which would drain the introvert's energy more, such as handling aggressive people. Differences can be a strength *and* they may lead to difficulties.

EXERCISE FOR EI COMBINATION

If you want an introvert to talk, you need to set up a comfortable, safe environment. Introverts can talk easily if they don't feel intruded upon, pushed or demanded of. However, they have no *need* to share so they need to be made aware of the extravert's needs without seeming to be required to respond, especially on demand. Take the introvert out for a quiet dinner with just the two of you, then bring up the topics you'd like to discuss.

If you want an extravert to be quiet, you may need to give them enough information or something enjoyable or interesting to think about that engages their energies. Maybe it is planning a dinner party with them (they do need group activity every now and then) or a vacation or a major purchase.

Interactions Between Sensing Types and Intuitive Types

Sensing types tend to focus on facts, real world data and the physical environment. Intuitive types tend to focus on possibilities, creative urges, and their hunches, which often transcend the data. The famous lines from Hamlet to Horatio are a beautiful example of an intuitive talking to a sensing type: "There are more things in Heaven and Earth, Horatio, than are dreamt of in thy philosophy." Why concern yourself with facts when the possibilities abound for creative change?

A sensing type might say back with much conviction "Seeing is believing." Sensing types would rather not concern themselves with abstract issues. There is so much to be done in the physical, real (to them) world. After all, why concern ourselves with what MIGHT BE when there is so much that IS demanding attention.

Misunderstanding is easy because what each "sees" is so obvious they don't expect their partner to see something else. Sensing and intuition are irrational functions not derived from logic but from the data as it is perceived by the observer. Sensing types will naturally describe many details that intuitive types tune out. Intuitive types will jump into the middle with creative possibilities that sensing types tune out.

So you can see a meaningful conversation between these two could be difficult; they might even pass each other like ships in the night, without recognizing the full presence of the other. It may be difficult to understand someone who is basically getting information from a different source than we are and who trusts and believes in his/her own way of perceiving. Remember though, that everyone has the opposite side in a less conscious way.

EXAMPLE: SENSING TYPES WITH INTUITIVE TYPES

We have found that those who commit to each other or marry at a younger age are often opposite on one or more than one function or attitude. In our practice we have more often seen intuitive men with sensing women. Intuitives tend to dislike the day to day routine of maintaining a household. Regardless of gender, having a partner who sees the need for, and who may even enjoy carrying out, household routines is quite a gift for an intuitive. Difficulty may come, however, when communication needs arise. The imaginary world is not always interesting to sensing types; nor is the factual world interesting to intuitive types. Some give and take is again required as it is with the EI interaction. Conversations to handle "real world" issues should be held periodically even if not a turn on for the intuitive. The sensing type needs to listen to the intuitive, creative dreamer and not discourage them even if their dreams seem impractical at times.

EXERCISE FOR SN COMBINATION

Set a task that requires dealing with facts and possibilities. Perhaps it would be planning a career change, moving to a new place, or whether to have children. Listen carefully to your partner's point of view. Is one partner too afraid of losing possibilities? Is the other's need to be practical cutting out options? Lay out both the facts and the possibilities. Then analyze each and assign values to each. See if you can agree on a decision that satisfies both people. If not, a counselor may be useful in this situation.

Interactions Between Thinking Types and Feeling Types

Thinking types mostly think and feeling types mostly feel. Therefore, if you ask a thinking type a question you are likely to get an "I think" answer; and if you ask a feeling type a question, you are likely to get an "I feel" answer. Thinking types want reasons, many even demand rationales, analysis, and logic in a conversation; feeling types want understanding, warmth, and harmony. Thinking types generally have lots of logic to support their premises, hypotheses, or ideas. Feeling types have values that support their positions. They often support their positions by making such seemingly simple statements as "I care about this" or "I don't care about that." So, in a conversation between a thinking type and a feeling type, the thinking type may turn it into a logic contest or, at least, a sparring match; and the feeling type is poor competition. A problem may arise when feeling types get seduced into trying to play the thinker's game without being equipped for it. As a result they appear to lose. Of course, all feeling types know they don't give up their evaluations based on their values just because a thinking type tries to reason them away. They just say "OK, have it your way,"; that is, unless they have a lot at stake or they perceive the thinking type to be attacking them personally. (The thinking type of course, is never attacking them personally—only speaking THE TRUTH.) In this situation the feeling type may be very hurt or rally to the defense. Suddenly the thinking type may find themselves on the receiving end of a statement which gets them "where they live." It is as though the feeling type has artfully designed a very short response to have an impact on the thinking type and has eloquently managed to say with a few words, "Now, we'll play my game." These statements by feeling types may be: "I really find you boring," or "If you're so great, how come you aren't better in bed?"

Both thinking and feeling are rational functions; each is a way of making a judgment. While thinking types are tuned into the logic and of a situation, feeling types are tuned into the relationship aspects and quick to pick up on coldness, hostility, detachment, preoccupation, and other such assessments of the climate in terms of its relationship tone. Equally accessible to feeling types are harmonious, loving, accepting, supportive "vibes", as well as the range in between. The *topic* is not the primary focus of the interaction; the relationship is. A feeling type might say, "I want to talk to you about this because I care about you," and not be interested in a solution or an analysis of what is being discussed. Thinking types can become impatient and critical in a descriptive discussion that doesn't seem to have a point or call for an analysis. They may even provide their best "thinking" on the subject and find it is not what is wanted. It can make them defensive about value-oriented discussions as they are off their turf in these arenas, and they may try to avoid such interactions.

But all is not negative. Feeling types go to thinking types for quick analytical processing and thinking types go to feeling types for warmth and acceptance. They have much to give each other. Remember also each has the other side (T or F) at a less conscious level.

EXAMPLE: THINKING TYPES WITH FEELING TYPES

Thinking and feeling differences are fairly easy to see once you are "tuned in." Since feeling, while a rational process, is not easily framed in terms of reasons, the discussions between these two can sometimes be quite frustrating. The feeling type's "reasons" are values—what they believe to be important in life, such as human rights. The discussion might sound something like one person (the thinking type) advocating justice and the other (the feeling type) advocating mercy.

EXERCISE FOR TF COMBINATION

A young person in the family has had too much to drink and gotten into a minor car accident while driving. The police have taken the person to jail overnight. The parents are out-of-town and you two are designated to handle the situation. What action will you take based on what you know? How will you respond to the young person who is not injured, but afraid and shaken up? The car has minor damage, but not enough to report to the insurance company. Will you each handle your part separately or can you agree on a way to do it together? Does resolving what to do bring you closer together or alienate you to some extent? What do you each say to the young person? Look back at your process when you are finished to assist you in future discussions where disagreement is likely or possible.

Interactions Between Judging Types and Perceiving Types

Judging types seek organization and build structures and perceiving types knock structures down, go around or under them, and generally prefer to make their own structures as they go along. This dimension is a brilliant formulation of Katharine Briggs and Isabel Briggs Myers, using Jungian theory as the base. It explains in a relatively easy way hundreds of differences that arise between people living together, such as: a regular time for dinner, meeting at the appointed time or within five minutes of it, hanging up one's towel neatly after a bath, putting things away that have been used. These examples are all from the point of view of the person who values structures and needs to complete certain tasks in order to be free for the rest of the day. They are organized, prioritize easily, and often do the hardest things first. They often have lots of "shoulds" for themselves and others.

On the other side, the perceiving side, is the person who wants more freedom and works the tasks in their own way as they go through the day. They want flexibility and do not want to be held to the letter of apparent commitments. They may call a friend for a quick message and get involved in an interesting discussion, meet someone exciting and miss an appointment, put off unpleasant tasks in favor of more intriguing ones, and/or have a messy house but a neat personal appearance. The phrase "apparent commitments" is used because perceiving types often have a hard time committing themselves to anything because they believe they will lose their other options. They feel trapped and confined by structure unless it is their own. They are often very efficient at accomplishing tasks they have set out for themselves. If *you* try to pin them down; they may elude you.

At their worst perceiving types can appear (or be) irresponsible and lazy, whereas judging types can appear (or be) authoritarian and demanding. Remember, though, both orientations are always there in each of us at different levels of consciousness. The judging type's *inner* world can be chaotic and the perceiving type's *inner* world may be ordered. The less conscious aspect of oneself can easily seem to belong to the other person.

EXAMPLE: JUDGING TYPES WITH PERCEIVING TYPES

A difference in JP is fairly common in the people we see. Judging types often pick up more responsibility than they really want because they "should." Judging types find attractive the apparent freedom of the perceiving type to do what they please. Perceiving types are more focused on discovery than responsibility. Perceiving types are often attracted to the judging type's apparent willingness to handle the "shoulds" of life. Each can see the other as controlling. One P man married to a J woman said she always straightened the towel he had been using before he even was finished in the bathroom. While they clearly loved each other, they were very annoyed with each other's behavior.

EXERCISE FOR JP COMBINATION

Plan a vacation together. Let the judging type take the lead with the planning by putting out several options of places they would like to go and things they would like to do. Let the perceiving type respond to those ideas by expressing interest or no interest. This format could be followed until the place, dates, and where to stay have been established. That way arrangements can be made ahead of time to satisfy J needs. Leave specific plans for what to do upon arrival largely up to the perceiving type and be willing to be flexible and spontaneous to satisfy P needs. If you cannot agree on where to go, see if you can decide to alternate your desires with your partner's by planning a later trip. An alternative is to agree that you can take vacations separately at times to do your own thing and together at times to be with each other as a couple.

Relationships: Tips for Couples

1. It is only with others that we can test out our behavior and see how effective it is.
2. It is only in a committed relationship that we are involved enough not to leave when things become difficult and primitive or undifferentiated personality functions emerge to cause havoc.
3. In some instances, what we "hate" in others may be an unconscious part of ourselves. Following these "projections" of our unconscious aspects, recognizing them, and integrating them provide a major way of working toward individuation.
4. There is some difficulty now with the concept and the reality of marriage because of the old role stereotypes. Chosen relationships in our time need to be equal partnerships whether in the form of marriage or not.
5. If the relationship has children as a part of it, marriage may still be the preferable form since the children may take the brunt of their parents' choice if their parents are not married.
6. The new age of the 21st century stresses both individuality and social responsibility. Finding some comfortable balance is a challenge for all of us.

Resources

Keirsey, David and Marilyn Bates, *Please Understand Me.*
Myers, Isabel Briggs, and Mary H. McCaulley, *Manual for the Myers-Briggs Type Indicator: A Guide to the Development and Use of the MBTI.*
Myers, Isabel Briggs with Peter B. Myers, *Gifts Differing.*
Sherman, Ruth G., *Psychological Typology and Satisfaction in Intimate Relationships*

CHAPTER II

Power in Love Relationships

"Where love reigns, there is no will to power,
and where the will to power is paramount, love is lacking."
—C. G. Jung, *Collected Works*, Vol. 7, p. 53.

Power Interactions of Love Types

Freedom to live one's life fully implies power. Power comes in many forms—it can come in the form of looks, money, position, charisma, intelligence, knowledge, wisdom, etc. When we talk about power between intimates, we are dealing with a very complex relationship. One person usually has more overt power than the other one. In a perverse way, the person who can leave the relationship easier at any given time—and it can change—seems to have the power. We say *seems* because the other person often has power they choose not to exercise. If there is a real and basic power difference between mates, one of two things usually happens—the relationship breaks up, or it is more like a parent-child relationship than an equal relationship.

Power and dependence/independence are closely allied. A careful balance is required. If we handle our dependency well, we can be close enough to someone we trust to allow ourselves to be vulnerable, cared for, and loving. (It is not possible to trust anyone completely, even oneself, since the unconscious factor always has potential to change things).

Paradoxically, it takes strength or inner power to enter into such a relationship consciously. To avoid intimacy is to be fearful, not strong. To be overly dependent is to be needy and demanding and is likewise not strong. On the independent continuum, it is well to be free enough to make independent choices when appropriate and to be able to have some control over the way we expend our time and energy. However, if we do not consult with our partners on the crucial issues or if we don't treat our partners as well as we treat our friends, the relationship has a power problem. There are many other ways power problems can manifest.

One person in an intimate partnership can "shut down" or "give up" if their perception is that there is little use to keep on talking. The other partner may not want to hear their point of view or may be so invested in preserving their own point of view that they do not listen. Difficulties with "shutting down" or "giving up" may also arise if one partner thinks that if they talk long and hard enough the other person will "come around." Other problems center on not really understanding what their partner is talking about or thinking that they already know what the person has to say. Overt power and covert power also play a part in communication. The kind of power you hold or exercise is related to your psychological type. Extraverts are naturally more demonstrative and often hold more explicit or visible power and communication. Introverts tend to be more subtle or implicit.

Power interactions can be very like a dance. Who is following, who is leading, and when do they switch—or do they change partners? In the following discussions, we will focus on power conflicts that are unresolved or unconscious, what happens when the partners have negotiated their differences, and what the dances look like. Some power moves are not deliberate, but a natural tendency of that type. These are often less conscious and less available for remedial action. They need to be raised to consciousness first, then remedial action implemented. Difficulties often arise when bringing unconscious material to consciousness especially if the individual experiences the information as negative. Denial and defensiveness abound in these situations. A strong charge on something always means there is something there that could use attention. If the person is ready to be self aware, and especially if the information is given with love and/or humor, positive change can occur.

The power to persuade, the power to intimidate, the power to seduce, the power to involve, the power to influence, the power to change minds and hearts, the power to express love, the power to provide hope, the power to bring serenity, the power to comfort—these are only some examples of how power can be used consciously or unconsciously in interacting with another.

The Extravert/Introvert Power/Love Dance

Extraverts are usually willing to initiate. Introverts are usually receptive to the other person's *input*. They may however not put out enough *output* to satisfy the extravert. In love, sex and communication, working toward balance is desirable. One-sidedness, while sometimes necessary, sets up unconscious energy which can backfire. Assisting each other to achieve balance is a challenging dance in itself.

If Unresolved or Unconscious. The extravert will come forward (strongly) and the introvert will back up. The extravert will get frustrated from lack of contact and the introvert will get angry (silently) from so many demands.

If Negotiated. The extraverts will back up and not fire such direct energy in the introverts' direction; the introverts will come forward and be willing to share more of what is going on inside and "where they're coming from." When introverts are safe, they come out. When extraverts have meaningful contact, they don't get all that energy backed up inside which turns into frustration and even anger.

The Dance. The *Dance* is two steps forward, two steps back—if the introverts will move forward, the extraverts can move back. Back and forth, to and fro. It can be done.

Self Assessment: Look at Your Party Behavior. When couples differ on this preference, many of them seem to encounter the following situation. Extraverts and introverts tend to react very differently to large parties. An extravert may enjoy being the life of the party, or moving around and making lots of contacts. An introvert may come in with sufficient interest and energy to enjoy the first hour, but they then start finding the energy drain debilitating.

What often occurs prior to counseling is that the partners start blaming each other. The introvert may see their partner as uncaring, selfish, and insensitive. The extravert may see their partner as controlling and "socially retarded." No matter what time they leave the party there can be recriminations. Even attempted solutions (such as the introvert subtly signalling the extravert that it's time to go) seldom work because there's too much payoff in the party environment for the extravert. Supposedly humorous comments such as "Oh well, here's my jailor again" can escalate hostility and bitterness.

It may help for the couple to go into counseling (probably short term) long enough to be aware that it's all right for them to be different—that one isn't right and the other wrong, one good and the other bad. It also helps to have someone else validate that the extravert-introvert difference is a real difference. One partner is not behaving that way just to annoy the other.

One win-win solution is to come in separate cars so the introvert can leave when the party becomes unenjoyable. Simply say "I'll see you at home" with a smile. A couple does not need to be glued to each other to belong to each other.

EXERCISE

1. List three qualities or behaviors you display that helped you to decide whether you're an extravert or introvert.
2. List three behaviors or qualities that helped you determine whether your mate is an extravert or introvert.
3. If you are the same (both E or both I), what have you experienced as the advantages of being similar on this scale? If you are different (one E and the other I), what have you experienced as the advantages of being different in this scale?

The Sensing/Intuitive Power/Love Dance

This arena is one in which it is quite possible to make the opposite type feel inferior. Intuitive types can feel lacking when sensing types point out obvious facts they have missed. Sensing types can feel deflated when they miss big, exciting, creative possibilities. Dancing well together needs both abilities complementing rather than combatting each other.

If Unresolved or Unconscious. The sensing type will take a *real* step and the intuitive will *imagine* how it could be "if only" . . . . Sensing types will be frustrated by the intuitive's need for them to be satisfying on so many levels and in complex ways. Intuitives will be frustrated by simple daily dance routines.

If Negotiated. This is probably the hardest dance of all in which to have satisfying contact for both partners. Stepping around each other may become one way to handle things. But, if the sensing type is not too bored by flights of fancy and the intuitive not too bored by everyday events, there may be a meeting of some fact and some fancy. Remember, the information comes from a different source. It is possible to do and dream, dream and do—it's good to have some of each.

The Dance. This dance is like do-si-do in a square dance since both partners tend to work around each other, But they can still stay in step—if they choose to do so, with some fanciful steps and some real down-to-earth ones.

Self Assessment: Look at Your TV Behavior. When couples differ on this preference, one may prefer to watch news, the other to watch imaginative stories on television. It is probably a good idea to have two TVs, one primarily for watching what is going on in the environment, the other primarily for escape into a fantasy world. If you decide to watch something together, are you accommodating the other person's needs or are you genuinely interested? As an intuitive, when do the facts get burdensome? As a sensing type, when does the creative process seem like avoiding the real issues? Some people think TV itself is to be avoided. On what basis is that decision made—too many facts, too much fantasy, too much avoidance, or what?

1. Make a list of detectives you've seen on TV, in the movies, or in books. Which ones do you see as relying primarily on their sensing functions to solve the crime? Which rely primarily on their intuition to solve the crime?

2. Also make a list of six individuals you know fairly well (family, friends, co-workers) and see if you can determine which use their sensing and which rely more on their intuition.

The Thinking/Feeling Power/Love Dance

Ask a thinking type what they feel and they will almost always respond, "I think I feel" followed by a word like *confused* which is clearly a head word, not a heart word. Ask a feeling type what they think and they will almost always respond "I feel" and give you their value orientation to the subject at hand, not a "head" response. They will tell you whether and how much they care about the subject. The feeling type will have as much difficulty telling you what they think as the thinking type does telling you how they feel. Because feeling evaluations and discussions of intimacy and tender emotions can make thinking types uncomfortable, they often put logic first. Because thinking logic can seem detached to feeling types, they often put values, and issues of harmony and relatedness first. It may seem as if both people are trying to lead, saying I have the "right" way to go about this.

If Unresolved or Unconscious. The thinking type will try to keep a little detached, and the feeling type will keep trying to get more involved and closer. They could look pretty clumsy with these differing needs. The thinking type will want to do it "right" and the feeling type will want to say, "once more please, with feeling."

If Negotiated. The steps each one takes to the same tune will be different. One set comes from the head, one from the heart. Since we all need both, it's important to let each person take the lead sometimes and show the other some new steps. Each definitely has something to offer the other if they don't decide that it's too hard to learn a new dance at their age. So, they need to loosen up and get out on the floor. They can dance together, since they do complement each other, especially if they can trust their partner not to bring out the "big guns."

The Dance. Heart to heart and head to head—sounds like a close encounter of the right kind.

Self Assessment: Look at Your Conflict Resolution Behavior. When couples differ on this preference, the thinking type usually has the advantage in a debate. The feeling type usually has the advantage in a social exchange. Rather than envy each other's abilities, this can be a time for the functional and constructive use of differences—to let each display the talents each has. Thinking types tend to be more competitive. Let them engage with someone else who enjoys that behavior. Feeling types can seek out a like-minded soul also. Watching your partner do something she or he does well that may not be one of your skills can even be useful in your own development.

EXERCISE

Think of a couple with whom both of you have had some problems. Express your point of view about having a dinner party and including them. Are there logical reasons for having them there? Are there values that would be violated if they are included? If there is a difference of opinion, will one person win and the other give in or what process will you use to resolve the difference? Are both people satisfied at the end of the discussion? Can you use your differences constructively?

The Judging/Perceiving Power/Love Dance

Perceiving types are usually clear about what they *don't* want to do. Judging types are usually clear about what they *do* want to do. If the judging types make their position clear, the perceiving types are often able to go along unless they really object. If they do object, it is then up to them to be clear about not wanting that alternative.

If Unresolved or Unconscious. The judging type has a definite way of going about things and is not always comfortable with free style. In fact, they will probably develop their own style within the free style. The perceiving type likes to go for the options, which may not make for a smooth gliding along together, especially if the judging type is unprepared or turned off by a spontaneous maneuver.

If Negotiated. There are definitely two different sets of steps here; it's really probably two entirely different dances. As a matter of fact, it *is* very hard to dance together. It's like the sensing/intuition dance, where there was an emphasis on different information. Here, there is a different emphasis on structure—one preferring more structure and one, more free-flow. Each can seem equally controlling to the opposite type, although the J structure is more visible and explicit. The control of P free-flow is less visible and implicit. Perhaps separate-but-together dancing is a symbolic way of dealing with the problems inherent in being with someone and at the same time being free.

The Dance. Couples can make up their own dance style. They're out there together, but they're each doing their own thing. Since no one is leading, no one has to follow.

Self Assessment: Look at Your Neatness Behavior. When couples differ on this dimension and are living together, there can be many verbal and non-verbal tensions. The J doesn't understand why, for example, picking up a towel and hanging it up neatly is such a big deal. The P also doesn't understand why it can be so important to have towels neatly on the towel rack. Each type may think the other knows "what I'm like and has deliberately chosen to do something to annoy me." This is an illustration of how difficult it can be to keep something in your consciousness if it doesn't fit with your natural style, even when that something may be quite important to the other person. That is why in couple counseling it is important to give each type a task that is equally difficult to carry out so one person is not carrying the responsibility for making the relationship work.

EXERCISE

Decide together what your standard for the neatness of the common living areas will be. If at all possible, arrange for each person to have a room which they can keep as they wish and are responsible for cleaning. See if you can come to agreement on the other rooms and how to maintain them.

To Recap
Dancing (Communicating) in Type

Extravert/Introvert E comes forward
I backs away,

The more E comes forward —
The more I backs away.

Solution: E back up.
I come forward (not easy for either one).

Sensing/Intuition S describes the here and now.
N describes the future vision.

S says be real; deal with the current reality.
N says be creative; change the future.

Solution: S takes the lead in dealing with the facts now;
N responds and gives balance.

N takes the lead in dealing with a creative future;
S responds and gives balance.

Both need to be patient, the future is with us longer than the present; but the present can be very demanding.

Thinking/Feeling: T says give me logical reasons.
F says give me what is important (values).

T may get cool and detached.
F may get hot and intense (or dramatic).

If things get very bad, T may get hot and F may get cool.

Solution: Don't try to play on the other person's playing field. This doesn't, however, mean you shouldn't try to develop your opposite. It means that: thinking types are often not good with expressions of the heart's values and feeling types are often not good at expressions of the head's logic. Explain to each other that your point of view is important to you and you want it taken seriously. In intimate relationships, a personal request of what you need is better than taking a position based on either logic or values—unless you both like to fight. If what's important to you is not important to

	the other person, it's better to work for solutions that satisfy both needs.
Judging/Perceiving	J says it's time to decide. P says let's be sure we've covered the options first.
	The more J persists, The more P delays. And vice versa.
Solution:	J takes responsibility to be explicit: e.g., unless you tell me otherwise by a specified time, this is the plan.
	P takes responsibility for speaking up about what matters early in the decision-making process or for going along with the program.

Power/Love Types

How each of us exercises power (and how we are all endowed with it) varies widely. Different types seem to have some natural, characteristic ways of exercising their power in relationships. It is important to find yourSELF and be yourSELF in spite of stereotype and social custom. Power also comes in many different forms: influence, intelligence, looks, character, strength in adversity, calmness in crises to name only a few; which ones are yours and which ones do you want in your mate?

In this chapter, dancing was used as a metaphor for how well a couple can stay in step, who follows or who leads, whether toes get stepped on, whether the same music is acceptable to both, whether one has to learn new steps or even new dances to mention only some of the possibilities. Each type can become annoyed with, or contemptuous of, the other's style. It is important to have a power base in reserve in a relationship, so your partner's power base does not intimidate you. The relationship agreement should never include a full-on use of all possible power, however. This means not hitting, cursing at, or deliberately demeaning your partner. If you're going to "lose it," call for a time out and demand that it be respected.

The following descriptions are somewhat overstated to make the point, so be sensitive not to use them to stereotype. See if the descriptions fit for you or your partner.

Thinking Types

Extraverted Thinking (ESTJ, ENTJ)

Extraverted thinking types tend to make their power explicit. They'll run as much of the world as you'll let them run. If you disagree, they'll probably argue with you, enjoy it, and maybe even convince you of their point of view. If you're not convinced you may just capitulate since they can be quite tenacious in their presentation. On the other hand, if you have a good argument, they can be very reasonable. If you don't think fast, the decision may already be made, because they're not only great thinkers, but they decide and organize too. Fait accompli!

Introverted Thinking (ISTP, INTP)

Power is more implicit for the introverted thinking type. They tend to get their power from having well thought out, reasonable systems that are difficult to challenge unless you're an ITP too. The problem is they may tend to identify with their systems; so, you may not be able to tell when they're talking or their system is talking through them. Their systems can be so well developed they may even pull you in and surround with their worldview. These types don't mean to dominate, merely to find out. Some of them may prefer to look at the data and figure things out that way. When they get it together, it's all so clear. They hope you understand; they don't like to explain. But, they will tell you once in concise language how it is and how it works. Knowledge is power!

Feeling Types

Extraverted Feeling: (ESFJ, ENFJ)

Extraverted feeling types get their power from their social ability and facility. How can you get angry with someone who knows your needs before you do—and fills them! It is the power of love and sensitivity. They have a good sense of humor and are good communicators, especially about feelings. They do like to have a good time while they're taking care of you, but then you enjoy it, too. If you express your appreciation, they feel well-rewarded. Of course, there may be times when you don't want to be taken care of; then this type's power can seem overwhelming or intrusive. But then, laughter and love can hopefully loosen things up again, and love *can* conquer all.

Introverted Feeling (ISFP, INFP)

Introverted feeling types don't relate well to other people's power concepts. As a result, they can sometimes find power used against them, as if to say, "pay attention." The power they have is usually internal and is a part of their deep caring and idealism. Introverted feeling types need to care, whether it's about an idea, a person, or a cause. Those with sensing are especially tuned into animals, children, and plants. Introverted feeling types' influence comes from this idealism, but they may be so distracted by the world of the ideal, that they can have difficulty seeing what's going on in the real world. Or they may see so much of a gap between what is real and what is ideal that they lose confidence in themselves. When they care, they are energized and motivated. Their impact comes from their pursuit of what they care about, no matter what the consequences. This may seem very confusing to you, but you do understand how important it is to have a dream, even it seems an impossible one!

Sensing Types

Extraverted Sensing: (ESTP, ESFP)

Extraverted sensing types get their power from their right here and right now ability to tune into what's going on and bring people together to deal with it. It's difficult, of course, if they're one of those people who need to be brought together. Who is an ESP willing to let negotiate for him—or her? That may take some thought, if it is possible at all.

Their adventurous spirit and easy acceptance can be intimidating. When they get knocked down, they can get right back up. They might be slowed down a little, but they won't let anything stop them!

Introverted Sensing (ISTJ, ISFJ)

Introverted sensing types get their power from the fact that they can be counted on. As a result they are entrusted with all sorts of things that might never be left with another type. ISJs are definitely responsible. This can be intimidating too. What if *you* goof up? What if you lose something they entrusted to *you*? But, then, they're realistic, and they do have a wry sense of humor. Maybe not now, though. Some things are serious. They'd like to be able to count on others, too, but you can definitely count on them!

Intuitive Types

Extraverted Intuitive (ENTP, ENFP)

Extraverted intuitive types get their power from—where else, their charm, of course. No one can be more energizing than an ENP who is in full swing. And swing they can—they're probably the swingingest of all. They can be down right intimidating with their wit and social ease. Humor—they invented it! Come on, when's the last time you had a good laugh when you weren't with one of them? Just their full attention can make you feel important. They're not trying to con you, they just know what you want to hear. The power of persuasion! The enchantment of the moment! All things to all people!

Introverted Intuitive (INTJ, INFJ)

Introverted intuitive types get their power from what they *know*. Just ask them, they'd like to tell you what they know, if you seem to be on the same wavelength. Talk about intimidation; they seldom use words like think, feel, believe, hypothesize. They KNOW. Do you want them to tell you the last insight they had about you? Maybe not. Sometimes they need to learn to keep their knowing to themselves. No other type looks deeper—but the assessments they make may not be made explicit. Just doing their thing—keeping in touch at that deep level that has meaning for them!

Positive and Negative Power/Love Behavior

	Power Base	Positive	Negative
ETJ	Explicit Understanding	Take Charge	Take Over
ITP	Implicit Understanding	Figure Out	Be Abstruse
EFJ	Expressiveness	Be Warm	Be Intrusive
IFP	Having a Cause	Pursue	Not Notice
ESP	Adaptation	Solve	Be Lazy
ISJ	Responsibility	Be There	Go Away
ENP	Enthusiasm	Enchant	Con
INJ	Insight	Inspire	Be Stubborn

Resources

Hirsh, Sandra and Jean M. Kummerow, *LifeTypes*.
Isachsen, Olaf and Linda Berens, *Working Together*.
Kroeger, Otto and Janet Thuesen, *Type Talk*.
Page, Earle C., *Looking at Type*.

CHAPTER III

The Types in the World and in Love

"Understanding, appreciation, and respect make a lifelong marriage possible and good. Similarity of type is not important, except as it leads to these three. Without them people fall in love
and out of love again; with them, a man and a woman will become increasingly valuable to each other and know that they are
contributing to each others lives. They consciously value each
other more and know they are valued in return. Each walks taller
in the world than would be thinkable alone."
—Isabel Briggs Myers, *Gifts Differing*

Know Your Life Type and Love Type

It is good to know what type you are and what type your partner is. With that
information you have an understanding of what your relationship is and
what it can be. We may be asking for a little more awareness than may be
comfortable; but after a while it will be a habit and you won't have to think
about it. Paying attention to the relationship periodically will pay off in a
more rewarding lifestyle.

You and your partner may have already taken the MBTI or have identified
your types in Chapter I. Now we want to go further on our journey with Carl
Jung, Isabel Myers, and Katharine Briggs to use all four letters in combination rather than one at a time. There are sixteen possible combinations of
the four preferences. In this chapter we are going to talk about the sixteen
types in pairs—as they were paired by Briggs and Myers. If you need to look
back to remember your letters, do so, and look for your type on the chart
below. Circle your type and your partner's if you know it.

MBTI/Jungian Type Designations		Jones/Sherman Type Designations
Extraverted Thinking	(ESTJ, ENTJ)	**Executives**
Extraverted Sensing	(ESTP, ESFP)	**Negotiators**
Extraverted Feeling	(ESFJ, ENFJ)	**Responders**
Extraverted Intuitive	(ENTP, ENFP)	**Charmers**
Introverted Sensing	(ISTJ, ISFJ)	**Dependables**
Introverted Feeling	(ISFP, INFP)	**Idealists**
Introverted Intuitive	(INTJ, INFJ)	**Innovators**
Introverted Thinking	(ISTP, INTP)	**Analyzers**

For a comparison with how other authors have designated the types see the chart at the end of this chapter. (Lawrence, 1979) (Keirsey and Bates, 1978) (Kroeger and Thuesen, 1988) (Elston, 1984).

Now let's proceed on our journey of the types. We'll start with Extraverted Thinking types.

Extraverted Thinking Type

ESTJ

Extravert • Sensing • Thinking • Judging

Being or Living with an ESTJ

ESTJ will:

- Want to be in charge of the relationship
- Be practical and realistic in making decisions
- Be more authoritative and possibly less sensitive to a mate's needs
- Be responsible and provide stability in the relationship
- See needs for romance as unrealistic—though they will bring gifts and celebrate birthdays, Christmas, and other traditional dates. The gift is more likely to be a plant which will last than a bouquet of flowers.
- Believe sexual fantasies are unimportant; the sexual act is taken seriously and is an important experience
- Be faithful to their mates if sexually satisfied at home
- Possibly get angry and then expect sex as a way of making peace—or as separate and unconnected from the argument
- See it as their duty to tell their mate or children what to do
- Know what is right for their children and expect children to live up to their standards
- Expect their mate and children to participate in community affairs
- Possibly unfairly place their anger on those most dear to them

They will value in their mate or children:

conformity • demonstrations of respect
cooperation • lack of emotionality • punctuality
warmth • appreciation for who they are

The Types in the World and in Love

Extraverted Thinking Type

ENTJ

Extravert • Intuitive • Thinking • Judging

Being or Living with an ENTJ

ENTJ will:

- Likely hold most of the overt power in the relationship
- Display a great deal of self-confidence
- Be articulate about what they want from their mate
- Provide excitement in the relationship
- Distrust compliments and not often pay them
- Believe sexuality is important—either as an expression of love or as a release from tension
- See discord over intellectual or philosophical issues as intellectual games and enjoy the games
- Probably remain committed and loyal in a long-term relationship
- Expect children to conform, be self-disciplined, and motivated
- Probably be surprised to discover some of their statements have deeply wounded their mate or children since they were not trying to be cruel, just honest and logical
- Detest inefficiency in both mate and children, and be verbal about it in an attempt to reshape the behavior

They will value in their mate or children:

intelligence • cooperation • competency
demonstrations of respect • warmth
self-esteem • appreciation of who they are

Extraverted Sensing Type

ESTP

Extravert • Sensing • Thinking • Perceiving

Being or Living with an ESTP

ESTP will:

- Love the excitement of risk-taking—physically, financially, emotionally
- Be confident of being able to charm others
- Be socially sophisticated, a party-goer
- Be skilled in manipulating a mate and getting their own way
- Hate being bored or locked into routines
- Possibly start projects and leave a mate to finish them
- Like and collect "toys"
- Not want to be "fenced-in" by a mate
- Have a difficult time apologizing
- Live in the "here and now"
- Possibly make a lot of money; possibly lose a lot of money. Finances may be on a see-saw
- Be realistic, not idealistic
- Enjoy sexual experimentation; and sex in itself is very important
- Be impulsive sexually and then have to be creative to get uninvolved
- Bring unexpected guests home for dinner, which is fine if the mate is also an ESP type
- Treat children as equals and not be unduly worried about their upbringing

They will value in their mate and children:

experimentation • follow-through • playfulness
willingness to stay out of or at least share the limelight
self-reliance • appreciation for who they are

Extraverted Sensing Type

ESFP

Extravert • Sensing • Feeling • Perceiving

Being or Living with an ESFP

ESFP will:

- Make any party a successful party
- Have had no difficulty attracting a lot of dates, and probably did the choosing in the selection of a mate
- Be stimulated by food, wine, clothes, travel, etc.
- Tend to be both realistic and spontaneous
- Need positive feedback from their significant others
- Be warm and loving without expecting much in return
- Be sexually responsive and playful
- Expend a lot of energy to avoid being bored
- Be sensuous in addition to being sexual
- Love to share the limelight—but also be in it
- Want romance to have an immediate concrete payoff; Romeo and Juliet were not this type
- Have a home that will look "lived-in," but tasteful
- Delight in allowing each member of the household to do whatever he/she feels like doing

They will value in their mate or children:

sociability • non-judgment • emotionality
optimism • appreciation of who they are • spontaneity

Extraverted Feeling Type

ESFJ

Extravert • Sensing • Feeling • Judging

Being or Living with an ESFJ

ESFJ will:

- Be loving and warm-hearted
- Be articulate about their own values and what they believe is best for the family
- Put a great deal of effort into maintaining harmony in the home
- Want a lovely home that is well-furnished
- Hate being criticized or given negative feedback
- Care about the rituals and traditions associated with holidays
- Be concerned about community affairs and want their mate to be also
- Want a lot of interaction with a lot of people
- Keep the home well-cared for
- Maintain stable relationships, especially with a mate
- Want praise and appreciation and will return praise and appreciation freely
- Possibly not be interested in experimenting sexually
- Desire and love children, who will be given a sense of family history and taught the "right way to do things."

They will value in their mate or children:

conformity • loyalty • predictability
responsibility • communication • appreciation of who they are

Extraverted Feeling Type

ENFJ

Extravert • Intuitive • Feeling • Judging

Being or Living with an ENFJ

ENFJ will:

- Be considerate and loving
- Communicate easily and well
- Be natural leaders of people
- Believe love is more important than power
- Be charming and have a wide circle of friends
- Be easily hurt by lack of appreciation or feeling ignored
- Be enthusiastic and stimulate mate or children into experimenting with new ideas or ways of doing things
- Be turned off by sex if it doesn't include romance
- Be sensitive, supportive, and understanding with family members
- Be affectionate and expressive with words and gestures
- Be able to move out of a relationship with remarkable facility once they've decided it's over
- Give freely but resist emotional demands
- Be supportive of children, sometimes to the detriment of the child's growth
- Have difficulty disciplining children or feel terribly guilty afterwards because they may overreact to the notion of injuring a child's self-esteem

They will value in their mate or children:

harmony • closeness • authenticity
imagination • appreciation for who they are • happiness

Extraverted Intuitive Type

ENTP

Extravert • Intuitive • Thinking • Perceiving

Being or Living with an ENTP

ENTP will:

- Be stimulating and ingenious
- Hate dull routine and manage to delegate it to others—a mate if the mate is willing to pick it up
- Take any side of an argument for the joy of debating, to the dismay of a mate who really values harmony
- Need lots of appreciation and admiration from both mate and children
- Focus on the future rather than the here and now—and because it appears to stretch on so endlessly, ENTPs may take on more than they can handle.
- Choose relationships with head more than heart, and move out of the relationship fairly easily (at least so it seems to the other types) when the relationship doesn't work
- Set their own standards for sexual behavior
- Want a mate to be at their own level intellectually
- Be willing to study means and methods of arousing a mate sexually
- Be willing to use sex occasionally as a release from tension, though generally preferring that it hold more meaning than that
- Be more interested in acquiring knowledge than money
- Be inconsistent in terms of time, energy, discipline, and attention paid to children

They will value in their mate or children:

independence • adaptability • competence
success • quickness of wit • appreciation for who they are

Extraverted Intuitive Type

ENFP

Extravert • Intuitive • Feeling • Perceiving

Being or Living with an ENFP

ENFP will:

- Be excellent at communicating and require communication from their mate
- Tend to be emotional
- Have enough energy for both of you
- Love romance—in every sense of the word
- Truly appreciate their mate's accomplishments—and communicate that appreciation warmly and with all the right words
- Be constantly searching for the meaning in life
- Possibly seem like a mind-reader to their mate, who will feel unable to hide anything from them
- Feel it important that everyone in the family take care of everyone else in the family
- Make their mate the center of attention during the courtship process
- Possibly feel deeply disappointed if the real partner doesn't match the fantasy.
- Probably continue to search for the perfect relationship either within or outside the marriage
- Be affectionate both verbally and physically with children and their mate
- Include romance and sexual fantasies in the sexual act
- Possibly be overprotective with children
- Probably be unpredictable in disciplining children—shifting from a threatened punishment to loving understanding

They value in their mate or children:

motivation • originality • imagination • communication
appreciation of the person they are • follow-through

Introverted Sensing Type

ISTJ

Introvert • Sensing • Thinking • Judging

Being or Living with an ISTJ

ISTJ will:

- Tend to live by traditional values
- Be responsible for any task they undertake and expect their mate to be the same
- Believe it's their duty to tell their mate and children what to do and how to do it
- Make decisions based on practicality
- Consider play a waste of time unless there is a practical reason (such as maintaining a healthy body).
- Want to be secure financially, but may never feel secure enough
- Keep a tight rein on children and expect to be obeyed and respected
- Participate actively in community affairs
- Probably be faithful to their marriage vows
- Want their home and furnishings to be neat, practical, and conventional
- Often be attracted to an opposite type and then try to "reform" the person
- Be willing to carry more than their share of tasks, obligations and projects
- Forgive a mate if the mate is sufficiently repentant
- Pay more attention to their work than their mate
- View sex as one of the rituals of marriage, take it seriously, and be grateful for the cooperation of their mate
- Be conservative rather than experimental about how, where, and when sex is to happen
- Be more comfortable with familiar patterns (going to visit the same friends, eating at the same restaurants) and may find it difficult to relate to a mate finding these patterns boring

They will value in their mate or children:

community-mindedness • morality • punctuality
productivity • thriftiness • decisiveness
appreciation for who they are

The Types in the World and in Love

Introverted Sensing Type

ISFJ

Introvert • Sensing • Feeling • Judging

Being or Living with an ISFJ

ISFJ will:

- Cooperate to the utmost
- Have no need to be in control in the relationship
- Likely to have a rather wry sense of humor which pops out unexpectedly
- Want to be secure financially
- Want to have some church affiliation and/or hold to some traditional religious values
- Be the worrier in the family
- Expect respect from their children and be dismayed by a child who does not want to conform
- Likely conduct a well-ordered home with everything in its place
- Be devoted and loyal to a mate
- Not mind undertaking all the chores related to housekeeping—cooking, cleaning, decorating—or yard, garden and car maintenance
- Often be unappreciated
- See sex as a necessary part of a love relationship
- Be unlikely to do much sexual experimentation as to where, why, how, or when
- Foster family rituals and traditions and create a sense of family history for mate and children
- Not be easily bored
- Need to learn to speak up about things that bother them

They will value in their mate or children:

thoughtfulness • adherence to tradition • religiosity
responsibility • practicality • appreciation of who they are

Introverted Feeling Type

ISFP

Introvert • Sensing • Feeling • Perceiving

Being or Living with an ISFP

ISFP will:

- Be a "private" person
- Like nature, sports, and animals
- Have the greatest degree of sympathy for others
- Want to please a mate and children
- Be pleasure-oriented in an idealistic kind of way—never at the expense of others
- Dislike any routine except those that are self-imposed
- Have their five senses well-developed—and be sensitive to sound, touch, taste, color, and form
- Resist conforming to rules and regulations, and not be likely to impose them on a mate or children
- Have a special affinity for understanding animals and small children
- Possibly have difficulty communicating verbally
- Likely have some difficulty choosing a career unless there is a particular talent in the fields of art or music
- Likely be very responsive to different forms of sexual stimulation that appeal to the five senses
- Often demonstrate a love of nature by filling the home with plants and animals
- Tend to be impulsive and live in the moment

They will value in their mate and children:

social skills • loyalty
love of nature • ability to be happy "now"
sensuality • appreciation for who they are

The Types in the World and in Love

Introverted Feeling Type

INFP

Introvert • Intuitive • Feeling • Perceiving

Being or Living with an INFP

INFP will:

- Be the most romantic of all the types—and have very high expectations of the level of intimacy in a relationship
- Desire harmony, hate conflict, and try to avoid disagreements unless basic values are at stake
- Be responsive in a relationship and delight in pleasing
- Have a tendency to live more in the world of imagination than in the "real" world
- Search all their lives for the "meaning" in life
- Become very cynical if they harbor too many disappointments and resentments
- Be articulate and want to communicate with their mate at deep, meaningful levels
- Need a room of their "own" to which they can retreat and regroup their energies
- Find romance and anticipation of the sexual act important
- Be naturally elusive in a relationship which will keep their mate pursuing them
- Be charming and gracious to those whom they choose to invite into their home
- Have a tendency to support their children against everyone else

They will value in their mate or children:

creativity • honor and ethics
real-world skills • need for harmony
self-esteem • appreciation of who they are

Introverted Thinking Type

ISTP

Introvert • Sensing • Thinking • Perceiving

Being or Living with an ISTP

ISTP will:

- Be adventuresome in their choice of sports and hobbies
- Be cool in their observations of life
- Be spontaneous
- Possibly have a tendency not to follow through on projects they undertake
- Be good at "fixing" things
- Be seen by their mate as uncommunicative
- Want to be right more than they want to please
- Not be likely to make any changes for the relationship, but may be able to get their mate to change
- Be easy to stimulate sexually via the concrete approach but not by the abstract or the romantic
- Not want to feel trapped or bound by a mate's emotional responses
- Probably have a plethora of activities in which they take part, many of them involving risk
- Probably be generous with their mate and children
- Often not choose wisely in relationships

They will value in their mate and children:

flexibility • lack of emotionality
love of adventure • self-sufficiency
appreciation of who they are

INTP

Introvert • Intuitive • Thinking • Perceiving

Being or Living with an INTP

INTP will:

- Not be likely to use frequent or profuse terms of endearment
- Have a tendency to be dogmatic, such is their faith in their own view
- Want to be seen as competent and want to be respected for their competence
- Possibly be the most brilliant of all the types
- Feel nobody understands them—and that may be true
- Sometimes be seen as cold or uncaring
- Be a private person even within a relationship
- Expect children to accept the consequences of their behavior and their choices
- Possibly be lacking in follow-through once they've intellectually solved the problem
- Probably not participate in community activities and projects
- Be cautious in managing finances
- Find sexual contact more meaningful than recreational, though that may not be apparent to their partner
- Not enjoy sex preceded by emotional conflicts
- Have no tolerance for their own mistakes

They will value in their mate and children:

ingenuity • competence • independence
intelligence • complexity • logic
appreciation of who they are

INTJ

Introvert • Intuitive • Thinking • Judging

Being or Living with an INTJ

INTJ will:

- Be quietly stubborn or persistent
- Be highly self-confident
- Want to get things decided quickly, and will make decisions easily
- Love challenges and be creative in responding to them
- Often be seen as a "General" by those in intimate relationships with them
- Often drive their mate or children as hard as they drive themselves
- Often be seen as difficult to satisfy by their mate and children
- Be hard to read
- Be sensitive to rejection, though no one may know that
- Be very selective about those with whom they have physical interactions
- Be devoted to their mate and children
- Be independent and value independent behavior in their mate and children
- Be perfectionistic whether at work or at play
- Want to be asked for their advice rather than impose it on others
- Insist their mate be logical and rational if they are to be convinced of their point of view
- Be fair, expect fairness in return, and may be angry for long periods of time if they feel their mate is dealing with them unfairly
- Be helpful to both mate and children in developing their full capabilities
- Be a skillful & competent lover
- Be seen as cold and demanding at times

They will value in their mate and children:

intelligence • competence • achievement
ingenuity • complexity • appreciation of who they are

Introverted Intuitive Type

INFJ

Introvert • Intuitive • Feeling • Judging

Being or Living with an INFJ**

INFJ will:

- Want to please, enjoy and need harmony, but not at the expense of their own integrity
- Always value achievement as part of their lifestyle—as a student, employee, mate, or parent.
- Possibly need closure so badly they do not see they are causing discomfort to their mate by pushing for premature decisions
- Be affectionate in their own way and at their own time
- Be among the most stubborn of all types—will keep the door open a long time, be forgiving and compassionate, but when the door closes that's it.
- Want the atmosphere to be warm and loving before responding sexually.
- Possibly have romantic fantasies outside marriage, but will be unlikely to act them out.
- Be deeply bonded to their children—even to the point that children may take priority over the mate
- Do everything they do intensely and to the max
- Need support and recognition from their mate; criticism will close them up, turn them off, and even make them ill.
- Need more variety and freedom than is provided by standard chores
- Dislike being overburdened by too many details—may ignore reading directions for the use of appliances, standard forms, etc.
- Have a deeply spiritual inner life which will be shared with very few—and only those whom they totally trust.
- Be difficult to challenge when they say they "know"

They will value in their mate and children:

achievement • intelligence • complexity
"real world" skills • imagination • loyalty
appreciation of who they are • spiritual, moral, or ethical values

**Since we (the authors) are both INFJs, it's probably more difficult for us to be objective about this type.

Special Note

Most of the qualities we value or desire in a mate are qualities we ourselves possess. Yet many of us, at least when we're young, fall in love and marry our opposites or someone different on two or three preferences—individuals with qualities quite different from our own. Then, when the honeymoon glow is over, we experience disappointment, resentment, or we attempt to redo our mates in our own images.

All of the types have valuable perspectives and strengths. Understanding and accepting our partner's and our own needs and contributions to a relationship—especially when they differ—enriches our lives and helps us develop the undeveloped facets of our own personalities. Having a partner who is supportive of your professional and personal growth is far more valuable than having a duplicate of yourself.

Mutual Usefulness of Opposites for Couples

An Intuitive Type Needs A Sensing Type:	A Sensing Type Needs An Intuitive Type:
To pay bills	To plan investments
To remember birthday dates	To plan original parties and gifts
To get them interested in sports and the outdoors	To get them interested in new books and new ideas
To help them take care of their body	To help them take care of their mind
To understand how ¾ of the world sees things	To not care how ¾ of the world sees things
To follow maps and not get lost	To make getting lost fun
To be practical and make sure their feet are on the ground	To be imaginative and make sure their head is in the stars
To find things that get lost	To keep an eye on the total picture

A Thinking Types Needs A Feeling Type:	A Feeling Type Needs A Thinking Type:
To help them understand how they feel	To help them analyze
To build relationships with other people	To be assertive with salespeople, solicitors
To value tradition	To have perspective on the whole picture
To make sure that the feelings of children, family and friends are taken into account when the family moves to a new location	To see the benefits in moving the family to a new city, state, or country
To learn how to be harmonious	To learn how to be independent
To deal with inlaws, friends, and neighbors	To deal with lawyers, banks, and contractors
To provide a warm refuge from a hostile world	To deal with a hostile world

Families of Origin Can Affect the Relationship

Your family of origin can have quite an effect on your preferences and how they develop. Jung believed neurosis could be caused by being pushed to respond differently from your natural inclinations. Many psychotherapists believe that "everyone marries their mother." We're among the group of therapists who believe that many individuals marry someone similar in type to the parent with whom they still have unresolved issues.

It is very possible that by now you may feel comfortable in identifying the types of the individuals closest to you—your parents, siblings, mate, children. Probably it's easier to identify someone on the scales of extraversion-introversion and judging-perceiving. Consider each of your parents and see if they were similar to, or different from, you—and what effect that may have had on your interactions. Are these interactions similar or different from the interactions you have with your mate?

Let us give you some examples from experiences reported by our own clients during our counseling sessions.

EXAMPLE ONE

Paul is an INFP—an introverted feeling type. He is a very creative, successful architect. However, his personal relationships leave something to be desired. He is now on his third marriage and is seriously considering asking for a divorce. Examining his relationship with his parents it became apparent that he identified with his father and had never resolved his relationship with his mother. His mother appeared (at least to Paul) as critical, cold, and demanding. Looking at the type descriptions, Paul said that she was probably an extraverted thinking type. Extraverted thinking (ESTJ, ENTJ) is opposite or almost opposite to INFP and might appear somewhat cold and critical to a very sensitive feeling type.

Seeking warmth and acceptance in his relationships with women, Paul appeared invariably drawn to women who aggressively pursued a relationship with him. Once he committed to or married one of these women they immediately set about attempting to remodel him in their own image. As we studied these relationships Paul was able to identify aspects reminiscent of his interactions with his mother.

It was too late to do anything about his first two marriages except to learn from them. But Paul's third wife, Gloria, was amenable to counseling to see if their marriage could be saved. Gloria is a very successful business executive, an ENTJ, who really does love Paul and who was willing to look in depth at the dynamics of their relationship. She would, however, often become exasperated over Paul's withdrawal from confrontation. Gloria's own mother sounded similar to an ISFP. She was a homemaker whose only enthusiasm was her garden. Gloria claimed a lack of respect for her mother and very little communication between them.

In our sessions Gloria learned softer ways of approaching Paul with her perceptions and needs. She also learned to verbalize her love for him prior to asking for some change in his behavior. At first Paul found she was being manipulative with no real change in her acceptance of him. But after a few sessions in which he was really able to "feel" her love, he became more accessible, no longer confusing her with his mother. A year later, coming in for an annual checkup both Paul and Gloria indicated the relationship was more satisfying. They said they believed they could continue to work things out.

EXAMPLE TWO

Another client who appeared to be affected by unresolved differences with a parent was Eunice. Eunice is an ESFJ (extraverted feeling type). Extraverted feeling types thrive on affection and approval. Eunice's father seems to be an INTJ (an introverted intuitive type). Successful in his profession (a university professor in engineering), he left the raising of his children to his wife (identified as an ENFJ) to whom Eunice related very easily. She was very close to her mother but was also hungry for more interaction with her father, whom she respects and admires.

Eunice is 29, a social worker, and has never been married. She is an articulate woman who was very confused by what she perceived as a failure in the personal area (her label). Despite the fact that she has been in a series of relationships since she was 18, none of them have culminated in marriage. Usually the male would retreat and terminate the relationship.

In looking at a number of these relationships it appears that she is attracted to men similar to her father in a number of ways. She is more attracted to depth (introversion) rather than breadth of interests (extraversion), and to those who are ambitious, achievement-oriented, and rather reserved socially. She sees herself as initiating most of their social contacts, and believed she contributed a great deal to the relationships, but wound up feeling unappreciated and abandoned.

Early in therapy we had Eunice bring in her father for a session. With a little bit of prodding he was able to express his affection for Eunice and felt genuinely distressed that he may have deprived her in any way. He was also able to describe some of the difficulties he had experienced early in his relationship with Eunice's mother, and how they had set about resolving their differences.

Following this session, Eunice was able to look more objectively at her previous relationships. She indicated that she had probably tried to remodel the very traits that first attracted her into a relationship. She also consciously decided that a male more similar to herself would more likely provide an easier, more satisfying relationship. In the last few months she has explored several relationships with men different in type from her father, and is currently becoming quite seriously involved with a fellow social worker, an extraverted sensing type (ESFP).

When you can find some quiet time, take a while to see if you can identify your parents' types. Then try to recall some of the issues you've clarified or those still unresolved. See if there is a connection between issues and differences or similarities in type. Also see if these issues are related to dynamics between you and your mate. You might choose to see a therapist for assistance in exploring this in more depth.

Personal Growth as Individuation

Jung believed that individuation is the goal of life and of counseling. Drawing on unconscious sources through dreams and active imagination as well as conscious interactions allows you to become ever more of the unique individual you are and have the potential to be. It is an ethical model, with choices made for the benefit of self and others, not for control or destruction. Controlling or destructive impulses need to be related to and acknowledged, however, to minimize their impact on your personality.

In the earlier part of this book we asked you to determine what your favorite function was (S, N, T, or F) and which attitude (E or I) you preferred to use. Your *dominant* function is your favorite function used in your favorite attitude (e.g., extraverted feeling, introverted sensing) and may be thought of as the "captain" of your ship. Next you develop an auxiliary function or "first mate" which is different *in every way* from the dominant function. These two functions (the two middle letters of your four-letter type: ST, SF, NF, NT), along with the direction of your energy flow (EI) and your attitude toward the outer world (JP) form your "type" and describe how your personality manifests.

Now we want you to look at the individuation or developmental process described by Carl Jung, a process that requires you to start dealing with your less-preferred functions (or what you might call your less conscious side) by midlife. Jung stressed the need to be one-sided in early development to get clarity about who you are as an individual—to differentiate yourself and know who you are and what you most prefer. This one-sided development early in life also sets up a complementary position in the unconscious which needs to be made more conscious beginning at mid-life in order to become more integrated and whole. What this means from a type perspective is that you work on your preferences early in life, and you work on your non-preferences later.

As you go through life you find it is more functional to be able to use all aspects of the self to maximize your ability to handle a variety of situations and people. In this development, it is often useful to identify just one aspect of self to work on for awhile. Taking on too much can seem overwhelming and resistance is natural. In addition, since our less conscious side is often configured in opposite sex metaphors in dreams and in internal process, the problem of relating to the opposite sex is ever present. The more integrated we each become, the easier the task. We hope delving into new places within is an exciting journey for you. Someone defined personal therapy as graduate education of the self. We concur.

Jungian psychology and the Myers-Briggs Type Indicator form the theoretical model on which much of our therapy is based. We use other models also, of course, but the meaning, depth and complexity of the Jungian/MBTI model provides us with the one we find most effective. Even if we do not articulate the model to our clients, the search for wholeness, for meaning, for higher consciousness, and for acceptance of paradox in ourselves and others may reach the depths where true healing can take place. We generally prefer not to use medication in our therapy, but rather we seek to understand the suffering when it occurs and make conscious the choices that are available. Let's look closer now at the dynamics of the developmental model.

The Four Functions

Sensing, intuition, thinking, and feeling are the four mental functions.

The sensing function relates to the five senses and information derived from the perceived environment (inner or outer) but not derived in a rational or linear way.

The intuitive function relates to knowledge and information derived from tuning in to a perception of the outer or inner world especially information derived in a non-rational, non-linear fashion from symbols, signs, abstractions or other often non-visible sources. Sensing and intuition are the two perceiving functions.

The feeling function relates to values and rational feelings, not emotional reactions and outbursts.

The thinking function relates to rational process and analysis, not daydreaming. Thinking and feeling are the two judging functions.

The combination of your favorite judging function and favorite perceiving function (ST, SF, NF, NT) form the core of your type description, and reflect your probable behavior.

The Two Attitudes or Orientations

Extravert and introvert refer to the natural direction of energy used to cope with life. For extraverts the dominant function is directed towards the outer world. For introverts the dominant function is directed towards the inner world.

Judging and perceiving refer to the choice of function which is turned on the outer world and the way in which it manifests in the outer world. Sensing and intuition are perceiving functions. Thinking and feeling are judging or decision-making functions. If you are a judging type, you turn your favorite judging function (T or F) to the outer world. If you are a perceiving type, you turn your favorite perceiving function (S or N) to the outer world.

Dominant and Inferior Functions

Type dynamics shed light on which functions are more or less consciously available to the individual. The opposite function of the preferred main or dominant function is the least accessible function for the individual. In dominant thinking types it is feeling and vice versa. In dominant sensing types, it is intuition and vice versa. This opposite is called the inferior function, inferior meaning that it is usually the least developed function in that individual. Von Franz (1979, p.72) says the inferior function is where devils can come in, but also angels. Jung hypothesizes that we may have more trouble with people who use their dominant in a different attitude from the way we use our dominant. In other words, we the authors, as introverted intuitives, may have more difficulty with extraverted intuitives rather than with our opposite type.

Awareness of your own dynamics and the differences between people in terms of their typological state of development has as least two potential benefits. Not only can this awareness make your individual life better through understanding and acceptance, but it can also mitigate some major problems with others. The chart below indicates the dominant and inferior function for your type.

Dominant/Inferior Functions

Type	Dominant Function	Inferior Function	What's Easy For These Types	What's Hard
ESTJ, ENTJ ISTP, INTP	THINKING	FEELING	Matters of the head	Matters of the heart
ESFJ, ENFJ ISFP, INFP	FEELING	THINKING	Matters of the heart	Matters of the head
ESTP, ESFP ISTJ, ISFJ	SENSING	INTUITION	Tangible things	Intangible things
ENTP, ENFP INTJ, INFJ	INTUITION	SENSING	Intangible things	Tangible things

Type Dynamics in Relationships

We are in accordance with C.G. Jung that all functions except the dominant function are used in the opposite attitude from the preferred function and attitude and are somewhat inferior, even "primitive" in nature. In discussing the introverted thinking type C.G. Jung says:

> The counterbalancing functions of feeling, intuition, and sensation are comparatively unconscious and inferior, and therefore have a primitive extraverted character... (1971, p.387).

The extravert-introvert difference has quite an impact on the way each individual behaves in the world. Extraverts are right up front (you might say in your face) with their preferred function while introverts save their preferred function for use by themselves or for use as a less visible function while interacting with you with their auxiliary (second preferred function).

Example: An *extraverted* intuitive (ENTP, ENFP) directs his or her intuition at you while interacting with you. An *introverted* intuitive (INTJ, INFJ) uses intuition "behind the scenes" while interacting with you using their less preferred judging function (either thinking or feeling).

Looking at type dynamically, the extravert has three *introverted* less preferred functions. The introvert has three *extraverted* less preferred functions.

Since most of us would prefer to use our preferred function in the preferred way (extraverted or introverted), the extravert is often more comfortable with another person or a group and the introvert more comfortable alone. This is also the way each usually prefers to make decisions and to re-energize themselves.

Having *three introverted* preferences can make an extravert sometimes uncomfortably aware of the inner world. Having *three extraverted* preferences can make the introvert uncomfortably aware of the outer world. There is an awareness in both extraverts and introverts of the demands of the other attitude. When young, the person may sometimes consciously avoid the other attitude, but at midlife the other attitude often becomes demanding. Jungian theory and our experience holds that it is preferable to be one-sided when young, but preferable to work on developing the other functions and attitudes as you approach mid-life.

What are the implications of this kind of development for a couple that stays together 10, 20, 30 years or longer? What is acceptable to both partners?

The impact of the mid-life shift in consciousness can be quite a wake-up call. We see more people between the ages of 35 and 55 for relationship work.

For a more in-depth discussion of the dynamics of the individual types, including how type develops, see *Gifts Differing* by Isabel Briggs Myers.

Reminders

1. The preferred or dominant function is the "captain of the ship."
2. The second or auxiliary function is the "first mate."
3. Only sensation, intuition, thinking and feeling are functions; the others are attitudes (EI) or orientations to life (JP).
4. The four functions together can be thought of as a family within each individual; the first and second functions are like adults leading the way, while the third and fourth functions are like children that need the adults' support and assistance to develop.
5. The fourth or inferior or "youngest" function can cause problems but also can help you reach wholeness.
6. At midlife you need to pay attention to the less developed functions to avoid a crisis or work through one which has occurred.
7. Your partner's differences can provide valuable data to help in your own development and in your tolerance for paradox and ambiguity.

Some Concepts in Individuation

1. Jung's term for personal psychological development is *individuation*.
2. The tension of opposites is necessary to become conscious; further consciousness requires integration of paradox and transcending opposites.
3. Masculine energy complements feminine energy in a way similar to any other pair of opposites. The differences cause tension, but also completion within yourself, or between you and others.
4. Transcending the tension of the four functions and integrating the paradoxical nature of opposites in general are the goals of individuation.
5. Things that are unconscious in us are usually projected onto others. That is, we see things in others (which may or may not be there) while refusing to see them in ourselves.
6. Making friends with the primitive, dark side in each of us reduces its power and allows for more personal freedom and choice.
7. The inferior function is the most primitive and darkest, but it can also be where "your angels come in."
8. If you find someone backing away from you, don't chase them. Give them room, but indicate clearly that you care, *if* you really do care.
9. Reactions are often places where we are stuck and have little choice. When you have a reaction, try to catch it before you act or speak, then give yourself a choice.

A Comparison of Type Designations by Some Authors

	Lawrence	Keirsey/Bates	Kroeger	Elston
ESTJ	Practical Organizer	Administrator	The Administrator	Executive
ENTJ	Innovative Organizer	Field Marshal	The Natural Leader	Top Dog
ISTP	Practical Analyzer	Artisan	Life's Pragmatists	Performer
INTP	Inquisitive Analyzer	Architect	Life's Problem Solvers	Philosopher
ESFJ	Practical Harmonizer	Seller	Life's Hosts & Hostesses	Super Salesperson
ENFJ	Imaginative Harmonizer	Pedagogue	Life's Smooth Talkers	People Pleaser
ISFP	Loyal Helper	Artist	Life's Artists	Naturalist
INFP	Independent Helper	Questor	Life's Idealists	Missionary
ESTP	Realistic Adapter to World	Promoter	Life's Realists	Trouble Shooter
ESFP	Realistic Adapter to People	Entertainer	The Fun Lover	Life of the Party
ISTJ	Analytic Manager of Facts	Trustee	The Responsibility People	Recorder
ISFJ	Sympathetic Manager of Facts	Conservator	Life's Loyalists	Man Friday
ENTP	Inventive Planner of Change	Inventor	Life's Challengers	Inventor
ENFP	Enthusiastic Planner of Change	Journalist	The Optimist	Entrepreneur
INTJ	Innovator with Ideas	Scientist	The Improvers	Originator
INFJ	Innovator with People	Author	Life's Inspirers	Psychic

Tips for Couples

1. The more balanced the personality, the more effective in dealing with the various aspects of life.
2. Extraverts need to learn to introvert occasionally, and introverts need to learn to extravert occasionally.
3. Intuitives must know the facts to be effective, and sensing types must not disregard the possibilities.
4. Thinking types need to get out of their heads to be effective in some situations, and feeling types need to balance heart with head to be effective.
5. Judging types need to loosen up and put "the evaluator" on hold sometimes, and perceiving types need to make the best decisions they can even if they have to close down other options at times.

Resources

Campbell, Joseph, *The Portable Jung.*
Jung, Carl G., *Psychological Types.*
Meier, Carl A., *Personality: The Individuation Process in the Light of C.G. Jung's Typology.*
Myers, Isabel Briggs, *Gifts Differing.*
Quenk, Naomi, *Beside Ourselves: Our Hidden Personality in Everyday Life.*

CHAPTER IV

The Types in Interaction: Extraverts with Extraverts

No One Else

No one else but you
Could fulfill my needs so well
The things we do, the way we play
The goals we set along the way
And yet, my dear, from time to time
I feel a certain emptiness
As though we were partners in a business sense
With quid pro quo, which makes me tense
And makes me long for the kind of intimacy
We've never shared
Can you meet me there? You see it's true
I want it with no one else but you.

—Anonymous

What Type is the Best Type for me?

People often ask us "What type should I be looking for?" or, "What type should I have married?" or, "Who would be my ideal mate?" How we generally respond is that there is no "best" type for you. What you have is a choice of the kinds of excitements, comforts, joys, and problems depending on the type with whom you choose to mate. *Every* relationship has the potential to be deeply satisfying.

We would like to provide you with some perspectives on the possible interactions of types, describing briefly the interaction when the relationship is working and when it is not. If you are now married or involved in a serious relationship, you can find your combination of types and assess whether or not you are constructively using the differences and/or similarities in type to make your relationship as satisfying as possible. Remember, too, that each individual brings his/her own history to the relationship—including interactions with parents, siblings, and friends—and that this and other factors will contribute to the uniqueness of each and every relationship.

In this chapter and the next two, we will indicate some of the advantages and disadvantages associated with any pairing of type. It is really important to be aware that with self-awareness, mutual respect and acceptance of differences any pairing can create a satisfying and mutually-rewarding relationship.

In deference to the greater number of extraverts in the United States, we begin our listing of combinations with extraverted pairings, continue with introverted pairings, and end with extraverted-introverted pairings.

Extraverted Thinking Types (ESTJ/ENTJ) Together

When it's working: Both individuals are likely to be achievers, with high standards for themselves and each other, and are likely to respect each other's achievements. They will meet each other's needs for punctuality, neatness, and order, will desire and be involved with social contacts, and will enjoy intellectual discussions, though their points of view may differ. They may even view each other as allies confronting life on separate battlefields. If either or both are ESTJ's, they are especially likely to be conservative, community-oriented, and stable members of society.

In lieu of evidence to the contrary, it is our impression that this pairing is unlikely to occur. There were no such pairings in our research study, and neither of us have encountered pairings of this type in our personal or professional lives.

Possibly one reason for this is that opposites do tend to be attracted to each other. And if, as Isabel Briggs Myers suggests, extraverted males do the selecting in relationships, they may be more likely to look for an introverted female who will listen to them, or a feeling type who will provide the warmth, encouragement, and appreciation that they may have not yet learned to express for either themselves or others.

When it's not working: When two extraverted thinking types disagree with either a perception or a decision, there is the potential for violent explosions (usually verbal) with neither party being willing to concede nor mediate.

Both individuals are likely to want to be in the limelight, and resentments may grow if the limelight isn't shared. There are very few shy, retiring, background people of this type.

An extraverted thinking type woman may be more interested in her career than in her home and children (though both would be well-organized); a man who has fixed ideas of how a woman "should" be, may grow angry and resentful over what he regards as competition with the male role, and may express himself both freely and frequently with pointed jibes and criticisms.

If the children born to this couple are also thinking-judging (TJ) types, they may cope quite well with the standards and expectations of their parents. If, however, one of the children is an introverted feeling type (INFP/ISFP), that child may require more encouragement, warmth, support, and understanding than either parent is easily able to provide.

Some Helpful Hints

Any relationship can work if both people want it to and are willing to make the necessary effort. It may be important to remember what attracted you in the first place and see if it is still there. It will not work however, if one person wants the relationship and the other one does not. The constructive use of the same personality style for two ETJs might involve appreciating each others' logical and organizational abilities, i.e., how smoothly they can plan and accomplish their goals. They should make a time and place for expressing *positive* evaluations of each other and their accomplishments. Although it's hard for ETJs to express appreciation, they do need it. Neither is naturally good at putting the emotional glue in the relationship.

The most helpful thing outside of work for ETJs is to have a resource for tenderness, warmth, and appreciation, since feeling is their least accessible function. They can handle a lot of other things very well, but without this resource, they may get stuck in a pattern of negative evaluations and emotions. Making a mental note to focus on the positive aspects of the relationship and express them will be a gift to each partner. More balance and harmony can be achieved this way. "It was great to see you pull off that business deal" or "You have such a flair for high level performance"—statements like these can help if it is hard to get out "I love you."

Extraverted Thinking Types (ESTJ/ENTJ) with Extraverted Feeling Types (ESFJ/ENFJ)

When it's working: This can be a very common pairing. Both individuals will be communicative, will enjoy interactions with others, be community-minded, and be somewhat traditional and conservative (the SJs perhaps more than the NJs). If the man is the feeling type and the woman the thinking type, roles with the children may be reversed, but that is quite in keeping with the liberalization of male-female roles and two-career families.

When it's not working: If the woman is the extraverted feeling type (and considering the percentages of males and females on the thinking-feeling scale this is more likely to be true), she is likely to desire and at times even to demand a great deal of interaction with and attention from her mate. If most of his energy is going into his career, he may be unlikely to respond to her needs, consider them inappropriate and unessential, and respond to her tears, anger, or overtures with logical reasoning or his own anger. Neither response will satisfy her and may result in an emotional separation within the relationship. The woman may then pour a lot of her energy into the children, her own career, into community efforts, or perhaps into a relationship with another man, or even a series of relationships. The man may seek solace with another "more understanding" woman while still maintaining the formal marriage contract or relationship.

If the male is the extraverted feeling type, the woman's career and success may instigate jealousy and competition if he is not as successful and secure in his own life-path. The extraverted thinking type benefits from development of sensitivity in relationships. Since direct knowledge of feelings is difficult, information gained through sensing or intuitive data can enhance sensitivity. Women of this type may have a more difficult time than men because of cultural expectations of warmth and empathy. If this marriage results in divorce, relatives and friends might be more supportive of, and sympathetic toward, the husband who may perceive "she put her career first."

Some Helpful Hints

These difficulties can be overcome if each appreciates why they got together in the first place—perhaps one to provide logical thinking and the other to be sensitive and responsive. Then, they may eventually learn from each other to be able to be both sensitive and logical themselves, as well as for each other. On the thinking/feeling functions this couple can complement each other. Since the least accessible function of a feeling type is thinking and vice versa, they can easily misunderstand each others' way of communicating and needs. Thinking types usually need to understand and feeling types need a heart felt response when problems arise. If each can ask for what they need in a way that doesn't alienate the other, we are a long way toward resolution. "I need" statements rather than "You didn't" statements can bridge the gap. "I need a hug" (EFJ) or "I really appreciate your being there for me" (ETJ) can help get them past some hard times.

Extraverted Thinking Types (ESTJ/ENTJ) with Extraverted Sensing Types (ESTP/ESFP)

When it's working: If this combination happens to get together *and* if there is a great deal of mutual respect, both partners will learn from the other, resulting in individual growth. Since both will usually be verbal and outgoing, both will express opinions freely. The extraverted thinking type will espouse discipline and commitment; the extraverted sensing type will espouse tolerance and fun. Both will benefit from the balance between these two sets of values; and so will the children brought up in this kind of household.

When it's not working: If mutual respect is lacking, constant battles may result from the extraverted thinking type needs to control and shape up this "immature, acting-out, unpredictable" mate. The extraverted sensing type in turn will *not* be controlled or shaped up, will find more reasons for staying away from home, for indulging in risk-taking behavior, and for not following through on "assigned" chores and responsibilities. There will be an increasing level of mutual frustration. If, in addition to this basic conflict, a couple of rebellious teen-age children are added to the picture, alliances will be formed between the teen-agers and the extraverted sensing type parent. The extraverted thinking type parent may even be seen as the enemy.

Some Helpful Hints

These difficulties can be overcome if the extraverted sensing type appreciates the partner's logical thinking and the extraverted thinking type appreciates the partner's practical approach to solving situations. Extraverted thinking types can benefit from more humor; extraverted sensing types can benefit from more recognition that actions have consequences. They can each add to the other's repertoire of behaviors. Growth for both partners can be achieved by complementing the other's style and at the same time learning from it. The perceiving type may learn to be more organized and the judging type to loosen up. "Come on, let's drop everything and go away for the weekend" (ESP) or "I read about this great restaurant, let's make a reservation for Saturday" (ETJ) are some ways of taking care of each other. If one of the partners is the intuitive, an extra dimension is added which requires being more patient with a different way of viewing the world, a way of facts or a way of possibilities. Factual people may *seem* mundane to intuitives; creative people may *seem* to fly around too much to sensing types. Each has something valuable to offer.

Extraverted Thinking Types (ESTJ/ENTJ) with Extraverted Intuitive Types (ENTP/ENFP)

When it's working: Communication and understanding between an extraverted intuitive type and an extraverted thinking type will doubtless be easier if the extraverted thinking type is also intuitive because they may be more likely to follow each other's thought patterns. If the extraverted thinking type is also sensing, communication may be more difficult, although the sensing of ESTJ may help balance the relationship by following through with details and practical matters that might otherwise fall through the cracks.

There probably will be a great deal of excitement in this relationship. Like the extraverted sensing types, the extraverted intuitive types tend to keep things stirred up and moving, and the extraverted thinking type will not be averse to lively debates, interactions, and involvements. If anyone can "handle" an extraverted thinking type, it's probably the extraverted intuitive type, who can influence, charm, and persuade with the greatest of ease. In return the extraverted intuitive type would likely benefit from the stability, organization, and discipline that the extraverted thinking type would contribute to the relationship.

When it's not working: Both extraverted thinking types and extraverted intuitive types, regardless of gender, tend to be power-types and are used to getting their own way (although the extraverted intuitive will be somewhat more subtle about it). Moreover, extraverted thinking types often exhibit a strong need to organize people and things in their environment. Extraverted intuitive types (or any NP) have strong needs for freedom and are likely to push back, rebel, or escape from any attempts at controlling them.

The extraverted thinking type is likely to be very critical of any uncompleted projects, lack of punctuality, and procrastination, all of which the extraverted intuitive type is likely to exhibit and to shrug off as unimportant. The home scene may be turbulent. Extraverted intuitives may also teach their children how to get what they want from the extraverted thinking type parent, and promote evasion and strategy rather than discipline.

If the extraverted intuitive type is an ENFP, the feeling aspect may modify the conflict to some degree because Fs do usually value harmony. However, the extraverted thinking type may devalue the harmony and see the ENFP as warm-hearted, but fuzzy-headed.

If the extraverted thinking type is an ESTJ, communication may prove to be especially difficult, unless the ENPs overcome their tendency to disregard any facts or details brought in to support the logic of a position that doesn't agree with their own.

It would probably be wise for anyone partnering with an extraverted thinking type to have their own authority problems worked out. If they don't, they may be unknowingly putting themselves in a situation which demands that they resolve any such problems. Extraverted thinkers tend to sound like authorities on whatever topic they espouse.

Some Helpful Hints

Few people are more creative than extraverted intuitive types and few more organized than extraverted thinking types. IF the extraverted thinking type can be creative about organization and the extraverted intuitive type more organized about their creative solutions, both will be happier with each other. The extraverted intuitive type can help the extraverted thinking type to lighten up. The extraverted thinking type can help the extraverted intuitive to focus and follow through. The extraverted thinking type should not make the mistake of thinking they can "shape up" the extraverted intuitive. Appreciation of their charm will get them a lot farther than any structured program they might try to implement. As an example, if the ETJ wants a budget, they probably need to manage it themselves, with the ENP having some discretionary spending money. "Let's take every Friday night and go to a different restaurant" is something that might please both—something one can count on (ETJ) with some freedom of choice and variety of experience (ENP).

Extraverted Feeling Types (ESFJ/ENFJ) Together

When it's working: This pairing should result in a loving home atmosphere, with both partners responsive to each other's needs, with both valuing harmony and cooperation, with both valuing social interaction, and with both being somewhat traditional in their values.

If both are intuitives, there will probably be long and frequent conversations about the meaning of life. If both are ESFJs, there will probably be more of a focus on day to day activities and possibly the accumulation of material possessions. In either case, this couple will probably be the center of a social group with similar values, interests, and goals. Their children, no matter what type, will be well-cared for, both emotionally and physically.

When it's not working: One area in which this couple may experience problems is in bed. Sexual attraction is often greater when there are differences, because the differences create tension and excitement. This couple may find they are loving companions, but neither has much desire to respond to or to initiate sex. They may also be inclined to sweep problems under the rug for the sake of harmony.

Other difficulties may arise if they have not developed flexibility. Two inflexible feeling type partners, locked into differing ideas, values, or goals, may find their differences seem irreconcilable because neither will be looking for a "logical" solution. Extraverted feeling types, when their feeling assessment of the relationship changes, are sometimes able to walk away from a difficult relationship with apparently no concern at all for a partner to whom they had been totally committed.

Some Helpful Hints

These difficulties may be overcome by appreciating what they have in common and working toward developing more balance with the other functions.

Sometimes by gaining more perspective the desired harmony can be achieved, and the excitement can still be kept. If the couple can maintain an underlying respect and appreciation for each other, then the conflict may enhance the relationship. However, if the couple find they are fighting all of the time, then they may need to get perspective from an outside source (friend, counselor) so they can learn new and constructive ways of solving their problems. It is possible for the couple to develop a routine that allows for relaxation and warmth to surface so that both can be more responsive and responsible. A movie every weekend with time for a snack or beverage afterward and someone else taking care of the children can provide the time and space both need to feel freer and more loving.

Extraverted Feeling Types (ESFJ, ENFJ) with Extraverted Sensing Types (ESTP/ESFP)

When it's working: In this combination, the extraverted feeling type will probably bend over backwards to please and accommodate the extraverted sensing type partner, for the needs of these two types will probably be very different. Living on the edge may provide just the touch of excitement an extraverted feeling type may enjoy. The extraverted sensing type will probably also tolerate and accept the extraverted feeling type's needs for stability and structure, even though such needs may seem unfathomable to the extraverted sensing type.

When it's not working: The risk-taking proclivities of the extraverted sensing type will be admired by the extraverted feeling type *if* they are successful. If the risks fail, the extraverted feeling type's need for security will be threatened. "Ought's", "should's", and "must's" will permeate the conversation, with the extraverted sensing type likely to turn a deaf ear to all the admonishments. The extraverted sensing partner may feel the need to make frequent moves, disrupting the extraverted feeling type's development of a sense of community.

Extraverted sensing types are less likely than other types to put up with boredom, judgments, or heavy disapproval. They could drift into another relationship if this is all they get at home. Since they tend to be charming and at ease with people, it is easy to get involved in extra-marital affairs, and the commitment expected by the extraverted feeling type may never quite be there. Children of such couples may feel torn in their loyalties and conflicted in their values.

Some Helpful Hints

These difficulties can be resolved if appreciation of each other's gifts can be rekindled. The fun and excitement of the extraverted sensing type and the loving responsiveness of the extraverted feeling type can add a great deal to a relationship if inner judgments or outer judgments are focused on the positive. Extraverted feeling types can be great salespeople, especially ESFJs. Extraverted sensing types can be great experiencers and "hands on" people. Both love social situations and the potential for fun is great. If the FJ organizes and the SP participates, life can be very enjoyable.

Extraverted Feeling Types (ESFJ/ENFJ) with Extraverted Intuitive Types (ENTP/ENFP)

When it's working: Excitement, warmth, and enthusiasm may permeate the home of such a couple. Friends will probably drift in and out—always feeling welcomed, always finding something interesting going on. The charm, the surprise, the unexpected gifts of the extraverted intuitive type may make the extraverted feeling type feel loved—which is generally a primary need of this type. In return, there will be expressions of admiration and appreciation, and the extraverted intuitive will respond to and bask in these expressions.

The extraverted feeling type can provide stability for the children; the extraverted intuitive type can encourage the curiosity and exploration that stimulates their growth.

When it's not working: Unless the extraverted intuitive type has developed some self-discipline, the lack of follow-through is going to create a great deal of anxiety for the extraverted feeling type. The very qualities that attracted the extraverted feeling type (such as the spontaneity and excitement) will pale in the face of what may seem like a lack of responsibility on the part of the extraverted intuitive. This might manifest as a lack of punctuality, unfinished chores, lack of involvement with disciplining children, not providing for the future, or not caring about commitments made to relatives and friends. The charm of the extraverted intuitive type and the freedom they seem to be able to choose can be a model for balance for the responsible and responsive extraverted feeling type, if they do not become upset by these differences.

The extraverted intuitive type will come through on their own timing, not that of their mate. The mate (whether male or female) may then turn into an emotional, demanding, critical parent, withholding the warmth and support they are capable of supplying.

Some Helpful Hints

These difficulties may be resolved if each type brings his/her best effort to the task: for the extraverted feeling type it is feeling responsiveness, for extraverted intuitive type it is creative charm. The judging type may need to be more *flexible* and the perceiving type more *responsible* to facilitate the interaction. Extraverted intuitives need a variety of experience and extraverted feeling types need a lot of appreciation. If the extraverted intuitive will tune in to their partner's world, they are capable of wonderfully appreciative comments—"Your eyes are like stars. I can see my soul reflected in them"—can make the day of the EFJ, while a trip planned to safari in Africa might be just the thing for the ENP. It helps to see your partner clearly and give them what they would like; not what you would like.

Extraverted Sensing Types (ESTP/ESFP) Together

When it's working: This couple will understand each other's craving for excitement and variety, be tolerant of any differences that arise between them, probably be involved in a great many activities, and share interests in sports and the great outdoors. There may be a continual turnover in friends, jobs, and homes, but this will be pleasing rather than distressing for both partners.

This couple will probably also live well, dress well, and entertain well. They like to live it up, but, if deals fail and there is a temporary economic drought, there will be no recriminations. They can easily move on to the next adventure.

It has been our experience that these couples rarely come for counseling. Perhaps as an extension of their dislike for sitting still in schools or libraries, the idea of sitting for hours being introspective in a therapist's office may appear boring and distasteful. Perhaps, too, they would prefer *not* to be examined, but rather experienced.

When it's not working: The variety and excitement that both enjoy might lead them in opposite directions. If neither is providing a stable home base but are out "doing their own thing," there will be no one to come home to.

This type may be more likely than some types to participate in recreational sex and in general do whatever appears available and exciting in the moment. Sometimes, however, what's "sauce for the goose" is *not* necessarily "sauce for the gander," and feelings of resentment and jealousy may result in an atmosphere of tension and anxiety. Extraverted sensing types usually prefer to leave rather than deal with anxiety and tension at home.

If there are children, their lives may be exciting. If the children are different in type from their parents and need quiet time, more stability, and more privacy, then they may not fare as well in the home environment. Extraverted sensing type parents may not deal well with what they perceive to be maladaptive behavior. They need to take action, not sit and reflect.

Some Helpful Hints

This pair can get through a lot of their difficulties since they both have a solid grounding in common sense. If they can focus on life and fun and not mind too much that some priorities may not be dealt with on time, they can laugh and love and enjoy. A minimum of structure and a division of responsibilities can also help. An open attitude and the willingness to be somewhat spontaneous when one of the pair needs to get away will add to the sense of adventure that makes them feel more alive and vibrant. They may also be able to work on projects either separately or together and bring their excitement about handling tangible reality to the benefit of their conversation and the relationship. These efforts can give them the energy to live through the more mundane aspects of their life together and maximize effectiveness of their natural abilities and inclinations.

Extraverted Sensing Types (ESTP/ESFP)
with Extraverted Intuitive Types (ENTP/ENFP)

When it's working: A relationship with this pairing is also likely to sparkle with excitement, although the extraverted sensing type is more likely to look for excitement in the moment and the extraverted intuitive type for excitement in the future. Both will want to be in the limelight, and may play off well against each other—leaving other couples slightly envious of the fun and activities this couple seem to share. If at least one of the pair has their feeling function developed, there will be warmth as well as excitement in the home, and both mates and children will feel loved even if expressions of love are sporadic.

When it's not working: Often individuals who are perceiving types enjoy order and neatness in their environment, even though they do not want to put the effort or energy into creating the order. Neither member of this pair is likely to want to be the one to take care of nitty gritty details, follow through on chores, balance checkbooks, make reservations, or make decisions. So life at times may be chaotic, with both partners blaming each other for the chaos.

Some one-upmanship is also likely to occur, for both types are accustomed to being able to get what they want. And the friction will increase if either one comes through sounding like a parent, for neither individual is likely to respond well to authority figures. Each may attempt to find ways to sidestep issues or manipulate the other to get things done "their way". Tolerance for the other will stop short of being "shaped up" to suit the other's needs. They are more likely to go their own ways rather than undergo what they would see as subjugation. Of course, with all their charm, neither would experience much difficulty attracting other partners.

Children in this pairing may suffer from lack of consistent discipline, from lack of economic security, and from lack of a parent rather than a friend or pal. When things are going well, however, they will enjoy the spontaneity and fun that can be theirs with these parents.

Some Helpful Hints

This couple has the benefit of both a factual approach and a creative approach to life if they each use their best function to help in the relationship.

Finding ways to appreciate each other while sharing the less desirable aspects of life can bring them closer as both would rather have fun than be serious much of the time. A minimum amount of structure can get the necessary details taken care of and leave more time for freedom to enjoy and experience life. ENPs can dream up ideas that ESPs can help bring to reality if they don't get bogged down in how to organize the effort. Letting each person contribute when he or she is in the right space to do so is more effective than trying to set up a schedule.

Extraverted Intuitive Types (ENTP/ENFP) Together

When it's working: All that charm under one roof? Enthusiasm, innovation, and activity will be the order of the day! This relationship will probably work best if one mate is an ENTP and the other an ENFP. Nevertheless, no matter whether they are two ENTPs, two ENFPs, or one of each, conversations should sparkle, energy should abound for new undertakings—and there should be no one throwing cold water on anyone else's inspirations. The opportunity for building on each other's creativity will always be present. Spontaneity and creativity is to be valued and nourished.

When it's not working: Here, as with two extraverted thinking types, we have the problem of two leaders and no followers. If a good idea should surface (and many will), neither partner may want to bother with the details of putting it into practice or seeing it through to completion. Until maturity has brought development of the other functions many a good idea can remain in limbo land.

There is the danger, too, of each partner's seeing through the other's charming ways and becoming increasingly disillusioned if promises are broken and commitments forgotten, even if both partners are guilty of the same thing.

Other relationships may be a problem too. The excitement of a new encounter, the fun of learning all about someone new—physically, emotionally, and intellectually—can be a very strong stimulant to someone as curious about life as an extraverted intuitive. Neither will experience much difficulty in forming new and varied relationships; this can be a threat to the primary relationship.

For children who require a stable home base, or who need to master self-discipline, this couple may provide neither security nor good role models. For children who can be flexible and adaptive to each new challenge, this couple can provide much challenge and a chance to experience themselves.

Some Helpful Hints

To make their relationship work and use their sameness constructively, this couple should divide the undesirable tasks, keep a freshness always present, and appreciate each other's creativity. They have the possibility of the most innovative, fun conversations of any type. Their wit and spontaneity can keep things moving fast and their ability to pun or use words well is exceptional. The relationship will be more to their satisfaction if they can use their lively intelligence to dispose of routine matters swiftly rather than resist them. This approach can be more effective than hoping the other person will pick up responsibility for those matters (or hoping those matters will go away if ignored long enough).

CHAPTER V

The Types in Interaction: Introverts with Introverts

Introverts Together

Perhaps because we're both introverted, the following poem really appealed to us. For us, it aptly describes the aspects of a relationship between two introverts when it is at its very best.

> There is within each of us
> A private place
> For thinking private thoughts
> And dreaming private dreams
> But in the shared experience of marriage
> Some people cannot stand the private partner.
>
> How fortunate for me
> That you have let me grow,
> Think my private thoughts
> Dream my private dreams.
>
> And bring a private me
> To the shared experience of marriage.
>
> —"Love Poems for the Very Married"
> L. Wyse (1967)

All introverts must learn to find ways and times to share what is going on in their inner world. Without an extravert to push for interaction or to bring interesting things to talk about, introverts can go for a very long time without communicating in depth with anyone. Although they do not always seek interaction, they need at least one person in their lives they can trust at a deep level in order to connect to the world outside themselves. The less safe and the more vulnerable they feel, the less they will share.

Another thing to be aware of with introverts is that their best and main function (whether sensing, intuition, thinking, or feeling) is directed inward for their inner use. Therefore they are dealing with the world with a less well-developed function, which tends to make them less effective than a more extraverted type in the outer world. It may also make them less direct in dealing with people and the world. It means that they are always processing in two ways—one which pays attention outside; one directed to the inner world. You might say with an extravert that what you see is what you get. With an introvert, you have only a partial view. Introverts understand this and attend to the outer world after attending to their inner world. Extraverts may find this dual attention annoying or frustrating. In a similar way, an introvert may feel annoyed or frustrated when talking to an extravert who gets distracted by someone interesting entering the room. Neither is intentionally offending the other, but each may need to give the other a little space for behavior that comes naturally to different way of being in the world.

Introverted Sensing Types (ISTJ/ISFJ) Together

When it's working: These couples are often seen by friends and relatives as "salt of the earth" people. They will tend to be consistent with each other and with those around them, participate to some degree in community affairs out of a sense of moral obligation, be conservative in political and economic views, and maintain family and religious rituals. They will also tend to be consistent in rules and regulations for their children and provide a stable home base for children. Whether similar to, or different in type from, their parents, the children will always know where their parents stand and what is expected of them.

In our study, we learned that SJs partnered with SJs reported themselves more content with their relationships than other combinations on these scales. Less ambiguity in rules and standards may result in decreased stress and more comfortable relationships.

When it's not working: When disagreements arise between couples in this pairing (as they do in *all* relationships), both individuals are likely to silently withdraw and stubbornly withhold affection, cooperation, and communication until one of them breaks the ice. We have known couples who were able to maintain a formal frigid silence with each other for several weeks.

Problems may also arise when children move into the teen years, particularly if these children are very different in type from their parents. Rebellious, acting-out adolescents may confuse their parents. Parents who feel powerless to control formerly obedient children may turn on each other and blame a blameless partner for not being strict enough, for being too strict, for driving a child from their home, or for allowing things to get out of control. Angry, wounding accusations are not easily forgiven by introverts, and, while the relationship may be maintained there may be a permanent rift.

Some Helpful Hints

Since they value a disciplined life based on facts, this couple can get through a lot. If allowed to balance each other, this couple can share handling the "real world" effectively and still have time for play. They may be in danger of getting stuck and thinking things are hopeless without the development of intuition to help "reframe the picture." They need to share and not close up especially when there are difficulties. Getting a new perspective from an intuitive friend can help. Their sense of humor can be one of their best friends when they are in touch with it.

Introverted Sensing Types (ISTJ/ISFJ) with Introverted Feeling Types (ISFP/INFP)

When it's working: Isabel Briggs Myers, author of the MBTI, and her husband Chief, are representative of this combination of types. Isabel would speak often of the necessity of valuing differences in styles, and allowing each other room for being different. He was an ISTJ; she an INFP. Introversion was all they shared in common. His attention to detail and ability to deal with the real world (S) allowed her the freedom to immerse herself over the course of her lifetime in the creation (N) of an instrument that would prove useful for thousands upon thousands of individuals, groups, and organizations throughout the world. The introverted sensing type can handle many of the details of the sensory world effectively. The introverted feeling type can assist, but needs to continue working toward their ideal goals. Then, the relationship may be satisfying to both.

When it's not working: At times in these relationships, we find strains and stresses occur when the J in the pair gets locked into the "shoulds," "oughts," and "musts" and the P in the pair gets locked into the "wants" or "desires." The J may become self-righteous and accusatory about commitments, chores, or obligations which may hold no meaning for the introverted feeling type. In reaction, the introverted feeling type may become evasive or rebellious and respond as they might to an overbearing parent.

Unless the same ideals are held, discipline for children may prove erratic and inconsistent, with children learning which parent to approach to get what they want. For instance, if it's important to them to get to baseball practice on time, they'll probably ask the J. If they want permission to drop a class and replace it with an art course, they'll probably approach the P. Since both parents are introverts, both may sit on their feelings of resentment at not having been consulted and let those feelings build a barrier between them.

Some Helpful Hints

Sharing and exploring differences can help this pair understand each other. With Ss valuing the factual world and Ns valuing the possibility world, a bridge is helpful in bringing closeness. If each contributes what they do best, all can go well. The love of nature and the world can help if both use sensing to gain information. When one uses sensing and the other uses intuition, as with the Myers, appreciation of the differences and realization of how each contributes to the other's well-being is invaluable. Introverts who use intuition would almost always prefer someone else to take care of the "real" world, such as taxes, car repair, and yard work. Introverts who use sensing can enjoy the visions and possibilities a more intuitive style can provide, such as creating a sensitive home environment and bringing fresh perspectives to daily life.

Introverted Sensing Types (ISTJ/ISFJ)
with Introverted Intuitive Types (INTJ/INFJ)

When it's working: Depth and sincerity, a sense of responsibility, and dedication are likely to provide strong bonds for pairings of these types. While the introverted sensing type may perceive the introverted intuitive type as somewhat too fanciful at times, a sense of loyalty and a desire to make things work may help the introverted sensing type to appreciate and sympathize with needs that may not make any "sense." The introverted intuitive type is likely to value the introverted sensing type's willingness to handle some of the details of life such as filling out tax forms, balancing checkbooks, or taking the car in for servicing. The introverted sensing type is likely to value the excitement of the variety of possibilities that the introverted intuitive is likely to bring up for vacations or lifestyle options.

Children are likely to be brought up with consistency, training in moral and ethical values, and with a concern for the community in which they live. If either or both members of the pair have a well-developed auxiliary function of feeling, there will be warmth, caring, and intimacy which may be expressed in subtle, undramatic ways that will be felt by both mate and children.

When it's not working: One danger for this pairing is an introverted intuitive's need not to be bored—which may lead to looking into other possibilities for exploration. The INFJ's desire for romance—candlelight, flowers, and violins—may lead to unhappiness if things become too routine at home. Introverted sensing types may also become bored or impatient with the introverted intuitive's apparent lack of respect for the obvious. The sensing type may be frustrated by the intuitive's constant focus on dreams and on changing things rather than accepting them.

A quiet stubbornness, too, may also create problems for this pair. Both may become locked into their own perceptions (which can be very different) and judgments about their perceptions. Since silence is easy for an introvert to live with, communication may be shut off for days. The children may be used to keep some communication open, e.g., "Tell your Mother she left the light on in the kitchen," "Ask your Father to pass the salt."

The Types in Interaction: Introverts with Introverts

Some Helpful Hints

Self-development and inner exploration can be an asset to maintaining this relationship. Both types need to introspect, but not get stuck in some of their own ways of seeing things. Each needs to stay open to the other's goals and support them, even when considerably different. It would be well to have a negotiated way of ending silences, although utter necessity may sometimes prevail. Intuitives can bring their flexibility to ending impasses, since they can often consider the many possible choices available. Sensing types are generally more accepting of the way things are. Acceptance of each other and new choices may resolve the impasse.

Introverted Sensing Types (ISTJ/ISFJ) with Introverted Thinking Types (ISTP/INTP)

When it's working: Introspective and analytical, the introverted thinking type is likely to maintain logical, precise communications with their introverted sensing mate—and if that mate is also a thinking type (IS**T**J), communication may be easy and two-way. If the mate is a feeling type (IS**F**J), the desire to help and care for the introverted thinking mate may make up for any difficulties in communication. Often lost in their own thoughts and their own system of thinking, the introverted thinking type is not always an easy mate to live with. But, since the introverted sensing type is not likely to require or demand much from them (certainly not nearly as much as an extraverted type might), the relationship is likely to work. Although the introverted sensing type's dedication to family and community may not always "compute" for the introverted thinking type, once the introverted thinker comes to understand that the motivation is "pure" and not motivated by needs for attention or applause, there will be respect and understanding.

The introverted thinking type may get happily lost in their own pursuits (work, hobbies, etc.). The introverted sensing type will hold down the fort at home and on the job, be patient and value the introverted thinking type for their different but nevertheless valuable contribution to the family and to the world.

When it's not working: Both the introverted sensing type with thinking (ISTJ) and the introverted thinking types (ISTP, INTP) are likely to have difficulty in the communication of (or even getting in touch with) their emotions. Introverted sensing types with feeling will be likely to know what their feelings and emotions are on a given issue. They may be unwilling or unskilled in communicating these feelings and emotions however. The thinking types usually respond to a how do you feel question with "I *think* I feel —." Once problems arise either partner (or both) may pull inside, feel misunderstood (which may be true), and become resentful and alienated. Discussions may be brief and to the point, and they may spend a lifetime together with neither willing to risk being vulnerable by revealing sensitive, hurt feelings. Children growing up under these circumstances will have no role model to follow in learning how to create intimacy in a relationship. They may also wonder why their parents are staying together in what seems to be a relationship with few rewards.

Some Helpful Hints

The practical approach of the introverted sensing type can complement the thoughtful internal approach of the introverted thinking type. Introverted sensing types who are also feeling types can bring some liveliness to the thinker's more detached world. The introverted thinking type will probably need to make some effort to respond to some of the more mundane tasks in a relationship in order for the introverted sensing type not to feel they are carrying too much responsibility in those areas. The introverted thinking type may be quite satisfied if their partner in the relationship also has the feeling function. Having access to feeling, even through someone else, can be very helpful to this type. Relationships in which emotions and feeling responsiveness are less easily accessed may have difficulty since the emotional and feeling components are what holds many relationships together. INTPs can become bored with more down to earth sensing types but may be so comfortable they are willing to stay. The introverted sensing type may become disenchanted if the introverted thinking type does not value some visible success in the outer world.

Introverted thinking types are often good at writing a "program" for their behavior—if they can get a model "program" in their heads, it may help. Sometimes it has worked for us to suggest, especially to male introverted thinking types, that they behave like a certain movie star. In one case an INTP's attempt at being like Sean Connery proved very helpful in changing his wife's current anger with him. He became more practical in dealing with some ISFJ concerns of his wife. Sean Connery tends to be blunt, to the point, and does not avoid the issue (or at least he plays such roles). When the husband was more willing to "stand there" and not retreat into a more theoretical explanation of the problems, the ISFJ and he were able to resolve some household and relationship issues. It is usually helpful, especially with men, to talk specifically in terms of behavior. "What am I supposed to do?" is often the question that an answer like "I need you to be more responsible" is not adequate to handle. Once an introverted thinker has the concept and the pattern, they can implement the program more easily. If each partner can express what they need from the other, specifically, communication can be considerably improved.

Introverted Feeling Types (ISFP/INFP) Together

When it's working: Shared values, belief in similar causes, sensitivity, and striving for perfection can create a beautifully harmonious relationship when two people of this type marry, particularly if both have worked through their own sense of insecurity and achieved a modicum of success in the real world. During the sixties and early seventies, we had many couples of this type come in for pre-marital or marital counseling, not because of serious problems but because they wanted their relationships to be as perfect as possible. The caring for each other was very evident, and the level of intimacy and sharing was very beautiful.

Couples of this type, possibly because of their own pain in growing up and feeling "different", strive to provide their own children with a feeling of being accepted no matter what the child's type may be. The creativity and the very deep sense of caring that they contribute as parents can provide a very stable base from which a child can operate.

When it's not working: Real or imagined hurts for this very sensitive type can create barriers between the two. A feeling of having been betrayed once they have committed to someone (and commitment is not always easy for this type) results in a loss of trust that is hard to regain. And no matter what the partner may say or do to try to make amends, forgiving and forgetting may be difficult.

In the face of possible conflicts, introverted feeling types are likely to withdraw or escape from the situation. And if both mates withdraw, issues will neither be confronted nor resolved. Problems that are buried are likely to result in underlying tensions and stress. Then each partner may turn to someone outside the relationship for understanding and intimacy, or they may search for a new partner.

Some Helpful Hints

If this type keeps the feelings and creativity flowing, the relationship can maintain a high level of intimacy. Few other types have the creativity or capacity for depth that these types have. They will sometimes need to talk things out, which is not always easy for them. Although they are similar they should not assume their feelings are the same about things, but check things out with each other. Their intuition can be helpful in bringing a freshness to the relationship to keep it lively and interesting for both partners. The partner with sensing can bring their sensitivity to reality. Supporting each other's ideals can also help.

Introverted Feeling Types (ISFP/INFP) with Introverted Intuitive Types (INTJ/INFJ)

When it's working: This is not a common pairing, for both introverted feeling types and introverted intuitive types are under-represented in the general population. It can, however, be a very satisfying pairing, for both will possess and value creativity in themselves and in each other. Family will be important to both, and there will probably be a mutual desire for close, intimate relationships and a lack of desire for partying and for a large circle of casual social contacts.

Intuitives do not like to be bored (and if one of the pair is an ISFP that individual will also resist boredom), so couples in this pairing will find ways to bring excitement into their lives, but an excitement that will differ from that sought by extraverted sensing types or extraverted intuitive types. Dedication to an idealistic cause, involvement with humanitarian issues, mutual delight in discovering a favorite new author or artist, finding new ways of sharing or playing together can all be a "turn-on" for a pairing of these types.

Children of this pairing will feel loved and supported (possibly somewhat less so if one of the mates is an INTJ—for INTJs tend to have very high standards and can be critical if those standards are not met). The introverted intuitive will probably be the disciplinarian of the pair, but the discipline will be fair.

The introverted feeling type is likely to be the more flexible in small matters, and will probably do more of the accommodating. But when a really important issue surfaces the introverted feeling types will stand their ground and generally be able to work out a satisfying compromise with their introverted intuitive mate.

When it's not working: The introverted feeling type's (particularly the INFP's) lack of interest in everyday routines that do not carry meaning for them may irritate the introverted intuitive. Household chores, checkbook balancing, filing deadlines, stocked grocery shelves, the details and routines of everyday life are generally distasteful for both types. The introverted intuitive type's internalized standards of achievement will motivate them to do their share, and there will be resentment towards a partner who is not equally motivated. If the resentments are not verbalized, it may take a long time for the introverted feeling type to become aware that their mate has become disenchanted with them. By that time damage may have been done to the relationship. Once the introverted intuitive has become convinced that their partner is irresponsible, uncaring, or untrustworthy, the perception may be hard to change. It will be difficult for the introverted feeling type to live with lack of approval coming from their mate, and they may turn to someone new for such approval.

Some Helpful Hints

If there are problems that begin to surface, both would benefit from sessions with a relationship counselor. Both are willing to listen to constructive feedback and to effect compromises. They are not likely to come to sessions merely to have the counselor shape the other one up. However, if each uses the sensitivity inherent in their type, this may not become necessary. The desire both have to make the world a better place through creative change can lead to admiration and respect for each other's choices. If respect and sensitivity don't get sidetracked by mundane demands, this relationship has great potential for depth and mutual satisfaction. No other type matches the insights of the INJs or the ideals of the IFPs.

Introverted Feeling Types (ISFP/INFP) with Introverted Thinking Types (ISTP/INTP)

When it's working: If this is a pairing that describes you and your mate, it can be a very comfortable relationship. The two of you share enough similarities to create understanding, and enough differences so you'll each be able to provide the other with different ways of perceiving and making decisions about the world. Neither one of you may want to have a lot to do with the structured world, however.

The introverted thinking type may more likely be the one to do the financial planning, to deal with economic long-range decision-making. The introverted feeling type will be more likely to be concerned with the emotional climate—for both spouse and children—and to provide an attractive, charming home atmosphere (though at times it may be neither neat nor well organized.)

Because the introverted feeling type will so desire harmony and because the introverted thinking type will spend so much time living in their own world, there should be few arguments. Those arguments that do occur will probably relate to very important values or issues on which both should be able and willing to compromise.

When it's not working: One roadblock this couple may meet is due to the need of introverted feeling type's to feel loved, approved of, and secure. And while the introverted thinking type may love and approve of their mate, there probably will not be many verbal reassurances of that fact. "Of course, I love you—didn't I marry you?" is not the tender kind of statement that helps an introverted feeling type to bloom.

Another danger for this couple may arise from a lack of communication, and a tendency to assume that they know what the other is thinking, feeling, or wanting. Since they do tend to see life differently and to have different needs, assumptions about the other are often off-base.

The Types in Interaction: Introverts with Introverts

Some Helpful Hints

Learning to be more demonstrative, with flowers or cards or funny little gifts if the words are hard to come by, can be an important task for the introverted thinking type. This is true no matter what type they are involved with, but especially so in this pairing. Although their perceptions differ, both members of the pair really do very much want to be understood by the other, and can work to make this happen. The introspection and depth that each is capable of—one in a feeling mode and one in a thinking mode—can provide a study in contrasts that enhances the total relationship if they do not allow the differences to be alienating.

Introverted Intuitive Types (INTJ/INFJ) Together

When it's working: This can be an almost ideal relationship between two individuals who intuitively understand each other, who value each other's goals and achievements and the need each has to achieve. They can meet each other's needs for punctuality and performance. They have strong bonds with their children, and are able to provide discipline as well as deep understanding to these offspring. Unfortunately, the pairing is rare, for there are few of these types in the general population. Moreover, those few in early dating and early marriages generally are attracted to their opposites.

Attraction to the "opposite" often indicates that the introverted intuitive is seeking someone who is more comfortable with and enjoys working with the real world, who moves easily around large groups of people, and who handles practical affairs with ease. This leaves the introverted intuitive time and space for their dreams, visions, and dedication to their personal goals.

If the introverted intuitive chooses to partner late in life or to choose a second mate after the death of or divorce from a first mate, they are somewhat more likely to have learned how to deal with the real world themselves. They may even enjoy doing so, and may then search out another introverted intuitive with whom to share their life.

The introverted intuitive will attempt to be fair, just and loving with children. They are likely to share similar beliefs in methods of child-rearing and not to accuse each other either of "spoiling" or being too harsh in matters of discipline. Secure in themselves, there will likely be little jealousy.

When it's not working: This couple may get together later in life. If so, they may already be pretty set in their own ways, and adjustment to another, despite the love, may prove difficult. Introverted intuitives can be "picky", can want to have things done their way, and since they "know" what's right, they're hard to budge. Put two rather immovable objects together and it may require a very artful mediator to bring these individuals back together again.

This type is probably more self-sufficient than any other type (except possibly for the introverted thinking type) and this self-sufficiency can prove to be both a blessing and a curse in the relationship. Two self-sufficient individuals sharing a life may sound ideal—being together because they love each other and not because they need each other—but all relationships require lots of adjustments. Each needs to be willing to risk being honest about any negative reactions. Avoiding unpleasantness could make them avoid each other.

Some Helpful Hints

If this pair of introverted intuitives can be persuaded to use their strengths to be clear with each other about what their needs are, it may increase their ability to be flexible. It may also lead to their own personal growth. Since they tend to have the same strengths and weaknesses unless one is a "T" and one an "F," they will need to use their intuitive powers to find the best balance between them.

It is also important to label resentments that occur, not perhaps in the heat of the moment, but at a time that is sensitive to the other person's needs. If things build up and are not taken care of, there can be an erosion in the relationship that may be difficult to repair. An agreed upon time to express any problems could be very valuable. Both have good memories for the very bad, but also for the very happy. Since IJs have a difficult time in general getting rid of bad feelings (good feelings are not a problem), they need to practice letting go on a regular basis. INFJs deal with the world with their feelings, but this is not their best function. This fact can distort the value of some events out of proportion and they need to consciously seek balance. The same is true for INTJs who are better at being "cool" about the world, but in any intimate relationship feelings are important.

Introverted Intuitive Types (INTJ/INFJ) with Introverted Thinking Types (ISTP/INTP)

When it's working: Again, this is an unusual combination because of the scarcity of these types in the general population; yet the pairing, if it occurs, can be satisfying. Both members of the pair will be very much inner-directed. Their own personal standards of integrity will be more important than the opinions of others and they will value this highly in each other. Devotion to each other and to their primary family members will predominate. Friends and business associates will take a very secondary place. Discussions, when they occur, will probably be intellectually stimulating. Each will ask for private time, private space, and be most willing to provide it for their mate. They can be fine as travelling companions, anticipating and exploring the new with great relish. The introverted intuitive may need to be the one to make plans and handle reservations, as little as they enjoy handling such details.

Probabilities are high that both mates have performed exceptionally well in school (except possibly for the ISTP who may have been diverted into hands-on types of experiences). Standards set for offspring will probably be high, but there should be little disagreement between the parents on such standards.

If the introverted intuitive type in this pairing is one with feeling, the climate may be somewhat warmer both for mate and children. The responsiveness, appreciation and sensitivity shown by feeling types is always welcomed by thinking types despite their own difficulty in the expression of soft and loving feelings.

When it's not working: Difficulties may arise for a couple with this pairing of types because neither type demonstrates much in the way of flexibility. When disagreements occur, as they do in all relationships, both partners will have a tendency to withdraw and maintain their own positions. The one who makes the first concession towards reconciliation may feel resentful over having to say "I'm sorry," because this is not easy for either an introverted intuitive or an introverted thinking type. Both have a tendency to "know" they are "right." They are invested in their position—whether it is in reference to a philosophical issue, an abstract concept, politics, or even the procedure for organizing household tasks. Both are likely to be working (for neither is likely to want the role of housekeeper.)

If any children of this pair happen to be born as extraverts, their need for interaction and parental involvement may be experienced as a serious energy drain by both parents. If they can afford child care or have relatives to help out, this may lessen the stress.

If this couple can *not* agree on major issues, a split may leave them unlikely to want to pursue another relationship.

Some Helpful Hints

Having others take care of the more routine tasks will relieve stress in the relationship. The emotional needs each has and which the children have may need to be made explicit. They should not rely on their intuition when it comes to others, but instead get their input. Being clear about their own needs and willing to express them before they get too big can go a long way toward avoiding problems. The introverted intuitives may need to take the lead in these discussions since introverted thinking types prefer to stay in a more technical (S) or theoretical (N) realm. The J tends to put the intuitive in touch with daily needs although that is not their preferred place to be.

Introverted Thinking Types (ISTP/INTP) Together

We have never counseled a couple who were both introverted thinking types, nor have we seen combination such as this among the many couples we have known socially. Therefore, our description of their interactions is more hypothetical than our descriptions of any of the other pairings.

When it's working: Conceivably two introverted thinking types might meet working as colleagues in a scientific laboratory, in a philosophy department, as researchers, etc. Each might then develop sufficient respect for the other's values and systems of thought that they would decide that a life together as mates would more closely fit their needs than a life with any other type. Their needs for perfectionism in articulating whatever they wished to communicate would meet with understanding from their mate. This would be experienced as especially satisfying after countless experiences of feeling like a "stranger in a strange land" in their interactions with other types.

Social life would be selective, for neither would desire interactions with large or diverse groups of people. But the friendships they did develop would be with individuals whom they truly respected or found challenging. The small and intimate dinner parties they gave would be stimulating.

If one or both of these mates are ISTPs, there will probably be more involvement in sports, hobbies, hands-on activities, and less emphasis on purely intellectual interests. This is likely to bring more life, more earthiness, and sense of joy into the relationship.

When it's not working: It is our experience that few can be more surprisingly dogmatic, more sure of their position than introverted thinking types, albeit often in a quiet way. If both move into a strong position at the same time on opposite sides of an issue, it is difficult to imagine what might ease so tense a situation.

Daily tasks—keeping the refrigerator stocked, remembering dental appointments, remembering to take out the garbage, initiating whatever social contacts (even desired ones), picking children up or delivering them to functions—may fall by the wayside. Both members of the pair may wonder at times why they didn't choose to get together with someone who would enjoy dealing with all these matters.

Since this type often expects to be misunderstood and may not discern well how they feel about the relationship, they may be vulnerable to falling into a relationship with someone equally intelligent, but also warm, appreciative, sensitive, and responsive.

Some Helpful Hints

Sharing intellectual interests can be a strong point in this relationship. Since feelings are not readily expressed by either person, having a group of friends, a spiritual life, or some musical or artistic expression that can help balance out all the thinking would be helpful. Later in life, each needs to make more effort to discover some of the more unconscious aspects of self. For these types, dreams can be a very good way since they enjoy introspection. These types can also benefit from having a good feeling type friend who can help them keep things in perspective. Introverted thinking types tend to spend so much time figuring out things that they are heavily invested in their own point of view. If they can come up with a model or paradigm which includes sensitivity to others' points of view, they can be more effective in their personal relationships.

CHAPTER VI

The Types in Interaction: Extraverts with Introverts

One Possible Extravert to Introvert Expression

Talk to Me

Talk to me. . . .
How can we solve anything
If you sever our cord of communication

What part of me
Hangs up the part in you
That I need most?

The "right words" response
The "touch me now" look
The "don't look like that" reaction

God, sometimes I feel like I cause you
So much frustration
Am I so difficult to understand
Do I seem that complex to you?

At least you have my words. . . .
No matter how they come together
They are *my* feelings, *my* heart

And they reach out for a corner of your mind
That you haven't yet closed
So that nothing I say will penetrate

And I hear myself saying
"Talk to me"
And. . . I hear nothing. . . .
And I keep talking . . . .

And. . . guess what?
I'm getting tired. . . .

—Author unknown

Often when people observe couples and comment that it does seem to be true that opposites attract, it is because of their differences on the extraversion-introversion dimension. It is true, of course, that differences on this preference are more easily discerned. It is also true that more people are aware of the concept of extraversion-introversion than of the other three preferences. Nevertheless, there does appear to be a strong attraction between opposites on this particular preference. Sometimes this attraction is enough to keep a relationship intact; sometimes it is not.

Our extensive clinical practice and the research we have done seem to indicate that the relationship works better if the male is the extravert, and the woman the introvert in these pairs of opposites. It may be due to cultural expectations that the male is to be more visible. Perhaps it is because women, and especially extraverted women, expect and demand interaction with their mates even after a day of work. Introverted males are less likely to wish to interact after a hard day at work. Introverted males may get their socializing needs met on the job and would rather dispense with the energy drain of being with people after a day at work. Whether it is any or all of the above— there do seem to be more problems in relationships where the male is introverted and the female is extraverted. This, of course, doesn't mean that all such relationships have problems. It does seem that the very qualities that attracted the introverted male to the extraverted female prior to marriage (her friendliness, out-going ways, confidence in large groups, energy level, and involvement with people and activities) appear to create problems after the marriage. Nevertheless, these relationships can be quite successful and continue to be satisfying to both mates particularly after they have developed both self-awareness and understanding of each other's needs.

Extraverted Thinking Types (ESTJ/ENTJ) with Introverted Sensing Types (ISTJ/ISFJ)

When it's Working: This can prove to be an exceptionally satisfying combination of types. The introverted sensing type is unlikely to challenge the extraverted thinking type's need to be in control, to be the overt authority figure. In this pair, the introvert's sense of responsibility and ability to follow through will please the extravert and evoke little need for criticism or complaints. The household is likely to function like a well-oiled unit: plans will be made and followed, checkbooks will balance, dinner will be on the table on time, savings will grow and be invested wisely.

There will be a great deal of consistency in the raising of children. Rules will be clear, and discipline for infraction of those rules is likely to be firm but fair. Children are likely to know where they stand at all times and what is expected of them.

The extraverted thinking type is likely to provide more of the excitement in the relationship—to lead the introverted sensing type into more growth-producing experiences than the introverted sensing type might have considered on their own; the introverted sensing type will provide an element of back-up and support that will allow the extraverted thinking type to move up in their career relatively free of problems at home.

When it's not working: If the introverted sensing type in this pairing is an ISTJ, there may be more challenges to the ETJ's role as authority figure. In addition, ISTJs and extraverted thinking types are likely to have explosive tempers which can get set off by perceived irrationality or irresponsibility, to mention only two examples. Where there is a lack of agreement on basic premises, battles may be long and stormy—until logic finally prevails.

Neither member of this pair is likely to express much in the way of appreciation or compliments. The extraverted thinking type is likely to distrust anything that smacks of "flattery." The introverted sensing type is not likely to be very expressive. More focus on what is working and more willingness to express the positive will help get through some of the rough times. Children of this pair may find their home base secure, but lacking in warmth. If the children are either insecure or rebellious, they may see their parents as bosses rather than loving parents.

If the extraverted thinking type in this pair is the woman, she is likely to be more ambitious and to rise further in her career than her partner. Whether this creates problems for the pair will depend on their own attitudes towards male-female roles. Some women may lose respect for what they view as a man's lack of ambition and turn to male colleagues or superiors. Some men may resent their partner's dedication to their careers, feel neglected and jealous, and resent teasing by their friends as to who is "wearing the pants" in the family.

Some Helpful Hints

This pair will probably have an easier time if the ISJ is also F. While two Ts can have good discussions, TJs tend to want to be in charge. If both are Ts, it would be well to divide the work, e.g., who is in charge of what. Developing sensitivity to their partner's needs as much as to their own needs, and taking the time and energy to balance out critical comments with appreciative comments can go a long way toward making a better relationship. Using their thinking ability to take care of their children in supportive comments rather than constructive criticism will also enhance their home life. Ts are so good at strategy and tactics. If they bring this talent to focus on how the relationship can be improved, things can work very well. One tactic might be "time out" if things get heated. Another might be a regular time to relax, enjoy the time together and drop the pursuit of goals for awhile.

Extraverted Thinking Types (ESTJ/ENTJ) with Introverted Feeling Types (ISFP/INFP)

When it's working: This is truly a pairing of opposites: the possibly most self-assured with the possibly least self-assured, the most goal-oriented, decisive, planning types with the most flexible, creative, and softest of types. We have seen countless pairings of this type among our friends, at workshops (especially among the military), and in counseling.

When it works, it's very good. The extraverted thinking type is comfortable in the world, successful, and is capable of providing a stable, secure environment for the introverted feeling type. Freed up from having to make it in the world, the introverted feeling type can use their creativity to bring aesthetics into the environment, to add to the health of the world through participation and achievement in the arts.

Both members of the pair tell us the extraverted thinking type is "the competent one," the one who holds the authority both outside and within the home. Often the introverted feeling type is unaware of how much power they themselves do have and how needed they are by the extraverted thinking type for their warmth and sensitivity, qualities difficult for the extraverted thinking type.

Children of this couple will be expected to follow rules established by the extraverted thinking type, but will be comforted by the introverted feeling type after being disciplined for infractions of those rules. If the introverted feeling type holds a strong belief that children should be molded through reinforcement rather than punishment, they will fight valiantly to maintain that practice in the home. This might take the form of praising desirable behavior and ignoring less desirable behavior or in general fostering self-esteem while avoiding criticism. They may withdraw and suffer silently when punishment is meted out if they disagree but are reluctant to interfere.

In our research, couples of this combination often reported themselves very satisfied with their relationships. Roles were well-defined, and there were very few power struggles.

When it's not working: As the introverted feeling type matures and develops a sense of their own competency, these marriages may run into difficulties. Whether or not they can surmount these difficulties will often depend on the flexibility of the extraverted thinking type to adapt to change.

As the introverted feeling type matures, begins to insist on being heard, even questions the dictates which were formerly lovingly accepted, the extraverted thinking type may experience this as a threat to their own self-esteem. If they respond by putting down the introverted feeling type with sharp criticisms (which they are generally adept at doing), they may succeed in keeping the relationship at the expense of personal growth of both partners. It is difficult, if not impossible, for introverted feeling types not to be aware of how they feel at any given moment. The fact that their partner may not be aware of how they feel is difficult to understand; it seems so obvious to them. They may give a response they would like from their partner which is to take care of feelings first. Or, they may go along with the program rather than speak up, but quietly withdraw their feelings and involvement. This is the last thing the extraverted thinking type wants, but doesn't always realize how to take care of feelings while getting their point across. For extraverted thinking types it means slowing down and looking deeper. They can use intuition if available or just take in the facts from the non-verbal responses.

Some Helpful Hints

If the extraverted thinking type chooses to offer their best thinking to support and enhance the self-esteem and productivity of their mate, as they might the development of a prized employee, initial conflicts may resolve themselves. Both partners can then be on a more equal and satisfying footing. The introverted feeling type can be caring and insightful; the extraverted thinking type competent and achieving. Both can respect and value each other's gifts. The introverted feeling type may need to learn to protect themselves from some of the wording and intensity of the extraverted thinking type's presentation style. The extraverted thinking type may need to use their analytical skill to assess what's going on and decide on a strategy or tactic to handle it well.

Extraverted Thinking Types (ESTJ/ENTJ) with Introverted Intuitive Types (INTJ/INFJ)

When it's working: This can be a satisfying relationship, for both partners are likely to be achievement-oriented, and to respect each other for their mutual achievements. A good match in strength, there will probably be more equality in this relationship than in relationships between extraverted thinking types and introverted feeling types or introverted sensing types.

If the introverted intuitive is an INFJ, there will be more warmth in the home for both mate and children; if the introverted intuitive is an INTJ, there will be easier communication, particularly around decision-making.

To outside observers, it might appear to be a typical extravert-introvert pairing, with the extravert in charge and in the limelight at social functions. Most introverts have little need to be that visible. If you spend a great deal of time with these couples, you will come to realize the respect the extraverted thinking type holds for their introverted intuitive partner. Often the extraverted thinking type relies on the perceptions and perspectives of the introverted intuitive usually given in private.

When it's not working: The need of the extraverted thinking types to be in control, to be in charge, may come in conflict with the need for independence, especially of the INTJ. No one can be more quietly stubborn than an introverted intuitive. Although the INFJ (like most individuals with a feeling function) will value harmony, it will not be valued at any cost. Their inner "knowing" will keep them from buckling in any controversy, no matter how loud or angry the extraverted thinking type becomes. The INTJ, who may not place a high value on harmony, is even less likely to buckle if a difference of opinion arises.

Many problems arise for this couple over the rearing of children. INFJs in particular, tend to be especially bonded to their children, and the extraverted thinking type may at times feel left out of the intimacy between mate and children. The introverted intuitive type is also likely to come to the defense of these children if the extraverted thinking type appears too stern a disciplinarian, and again the extraverted thinker will be made to feel like the outsider.

In this pairing, it is especially important for the extraverted thinking types to learn to curb their tempers. Comments made in anger that sting or wound the introverted intuitive types (particularly the INFJ) are never forgotten nor often forgiven, and the extraverted thinker may hear 20 years later of the hurt they inflicted in a stressful moment. "My God, you have the memory of an elephant!" is not an unusual comment made to the introverted intuitive type.

Most introverts do tend to take longer to get over hurt or angry feelings. Extraverts are more likely to ventilate and forget. This seems to be especially true for extraverted thinking-introverted intuitive partners.

Some Helpful Hints

Introverts tend to draw energy in and hold it, mull it over, reflect on it; extraverts tend to collect information from everyone they meet and share it. The difficulty in "letting go" for an introvert is a real one; for an extravert it is a natural easy process. This pair, as well as the extraverted thinking-introverted feeling pair need to pay attention to what is put out and what is taken in. If the extraverted thinker can be somewhat less critical and the introverted intuitive less sensitive, they have a better chance of keeping the feelings in a good place. FJ tends to want harmony; TJ tends to want resolution. If both can be achieved by discussion and implementation, the possibilities of this pairing have great potential. Extraverted thinking types tend to get Is moving and more involved in the environment; introverted intuitives can supply careful attention to the Es ideas and insightful or factual alternatives.

Extraverted Thinking Types (ESTJ/ENTJ) with Introverted Thinking Types (ISTP/INTP)

If you have difficulty conceptualizing this pairing of types, perhaps it would be helpful to think of a highly successful executive married to a college professor of philosophy or economics, or of a surgeon married to a hospital administrator. Of course, if you and your mate *are* this combination of types you will experience no difficulty fantasizing an extraverted thinking type living with an introverted thinking type.

When it's working: Careers for both individuals in this relationship may take priority over family, and it may not be until the woman is approaching her forties that the couple will discuss seriously the option of having a baby.

Achievement in their own choice of careers will enable each individual to develop self-confidence and to be sufficiently secure in their own right to admire and respect their mate's achievements even in totally diverse fields. Two substantial incomes will allow them to fulfill many of their personal dreams, whether of travel, fancy cars, substantial homes, expensive hobbies, etc. If there are differences in their personal dreams, their logic should enable them to work out mutually satisfying options: "Yes, it's fine for you to take a three-week fishing trip in Canada—I'd rather fly to Hong Kong during that time and go on a shopping binge."

When it's not working: Introverted thinking types at times can be dreamers, crank geniuses, never quite able to make it in the real world. If this happens, their extraverted thinking type mate may lose respect. Their sarcastic jibes and put-downs may alienate the less successful member of the pair.

Even when both are successful, difficulties may arise—the extravert will undoubtedly want to socialize more, especially with those with whom they are associated professionally. The introvert may resent being "dragged out" to functions where there is no one with whom they have anything in common. Since they dislike "small talk," such an event will be considered a waste of their time—time they could use more productively in their own pursuits. And introverted thinking types have their own methods of expressing their resentments, whether by withdrawing, using "silent treatments," or possibly withholding sex.

Children of these relationships will probably be provided with all the material advantages possible—nannies, private schools, etc. Often arriving late in the course of the marriage, children are likely to be doted on by both parents and grandparents. The most serious side-effect of bringing a child or children into this relationship may occur if the child is a non-achiever or if the parents have differing views on child-rearing. In the first case, there may be a lot of blaming; in the second case, there may be out-and-out battles because neither the extraverted thinking type nor the introverted thinking type tend to be mediating, conciliatory types.

Some Helpful Hints

Two individuals whose primary function in "thinking" can lead a very stimulating life with each other. Remembering that "thinkers" enjoy debates, often caring little which side they take, many aspects of life can be explored and each may clarify for themselves what they actually do believe as a result of this process. Harmony is not a prerequisite for this pairing of types; mental stimulation is.

Extraverted Feeling Types (ESFJ/ENFJ) with Introverted Sensing Types (ISTJ/ISFJ)

When it's working: This can often be a fairly comfortable type of relationship to be in, especially if you are comfortable with structure. Any of the four combinations contain two Js, so needs for order, punctuality, and planning should be satisfied. Extraverted feeling types tend to be in jobs that allow for interactions during the day in the role of teacher, minister, counselor, etc. Quiet evenings at home with an introverted mate can then be attractive, even for an extravert. The introverted sensing type partner will definitely be ready for some quiet time especially if she or he has a job which calls for some extraverted behavior. In fact, this partner may want time alone even before time together. The ISJ partner will appreciate their mate's involvement with the children, warmth, and demonstrations of affection. The EFJ will appreciate the security, stability and follow through provided by the ISJ partner. Each partner in this relationship will most likely respect the other and count on them to be responsible. Stability and security are typically important values for both.

When it's not working: Extraverted feeling types tend to need a constant flow of strokes, and compliments do not flow easily from introverted sensing types. This can make the EFJ feel unhappy and not valued. The EFJ partner, feeling unhappy and not valued, may then decide to put the major portion of their time and energy into a job or volunteer work where appreciation is more readily available.

Other problems may arise if the EFJ is either in a career which permits minimal interactions with others or is "stuck" at home with small children. In either case, there may be more needs for socializing than the ISJ cares for and resentments towards each other for the lack of similarity in needs may escalate.

Some Helpful Hints

Two Js need to focus their desire for an orderly outer world on making things work smoothly between them. They may need to free up from making "judgments" and substitute accurate evaluations and acceptance. Js usually have opinions about the outer world that may be "right" for them, but not necessarily for others. Feelings need to be dealt with as they arise, with the extravert not seeming too pushy or the introvert too reticent. Both types need to build some fun into their normally very responsible styles. These types can handle the world, but also need to take care of each other.

Extraverted Feeling Types (ESFJ/ENFJ) with Introverted Feeling Types (ISFP/INFP)

When it's working: Since any combination of these pairs will contain two feeling types, there should always be a good degree of warmth in the household, expressed towards each other and especially towards the children. Sensitivity to the other's hurt feelings and a desire to make amends will especially benefit the introverted feeling type, who generally does need to be treated with tender loving care. If anyone can help the introverted feeling type to feel sufficiently secure to pursue and attain their goals, it may be the extraverted feeling type.

The introverted feeling type, in turn, will provide the extraverted feeling type with a listening ear. The introvert may also help the extravert to balance their social needs with a more humanitarian and broader perspective.

Even if the offspring of this combination of types are thinking types, there will be sufficient love and allowance for differences to permit the children to develop in healthy ways.

When it's not working: Jung indicated that the greatest misunderstandings may occur between two individuals with the same primary function (feeling in this case) if the function is extraverted in one and introverted in the other. Conflicts do occur in every relationship, and when they do for this couple, the extravert will want to talk it out *now*! Extraverted feeling types do need to get their reactions out—they can't sleep until they do. Introverted feeling types, on the other hand, will have a tendency to withdraw. Trying to handle their own reactions along with listening to their partner's is sometimes more than they can handle.

Money problems can sometimes sabotage this couple's relationship. Extraverted feeling types tend to have more "real world" needs; whereas, if the introverted feeling types have identified and are pursuing their goals, they are much less likely to be interested in financial returns.

Some Helpful Hints

Since harmony is so important to both types, it is crucial this area get a good bit of attention. The extraverted feeling type needs to be sure to ask for and listen to the introverted feeling type's response. The introverted feeling type needs to be willing to share values and reactions. Introverted feeling types who keep reactions to themselves, often with good intent not wanting to cause unpleasant interactions, can unconsciously build up a reservoir of negativity which can seriously affect the relationship by a kind of gradual withdrawal. Being willing to air grievances and work them out is necessary to the well-being of the relationship. If the introvert is willing to talk, the extravert needs to be willing to listen attentively. Introverts who are not heard may stop talking and eventually just leave.

Extraverted Feeling Types (ESFJ/ENFJ)
with Introverted Intuitive Types (INTJ/INFJ)

When it's working: This combination can work better if the pair is an ENFJ with an INFJ, especially if the extravert is the male. Values, goals, and modes of action would be similar, and the difference in extraversion-introversion could add sparkle to the relationship. Children would be raised with love and discipline. An appreciation of each other's integrity would add depth to the relationship.

In any of the combinations of these types, the J aspect of their types should ease many of the minor problems couples tend to encounter. Plans that are made will be followed, chores will be done; no one will be kept waiting without a very good excuse.

The extraverted feeling type's desire to please and to have harmony in the home should ease many potentially divisive situations. If you're aware your partner has your best interests at heart and is your ally, any INJ stubbornness should melt away.

When it's not working: One possibly difficult combination of these types is an ESFJ with an INTJ. This is not an unusual combination. The social skills and humor of the extraverted feeling type can enhance the goal-directed behavior of the introverted intuitive who tends to be more serious and persistent. There may be mutual respect and admiration for the part each is playing in attaining a satisfying lifestyle. But, an INTJ can be very undemonstrative; and an ESFJ usually requires more in the way of interaction and appreciation than an INTJ naturally provides.

If the extraverted feeling type turns their attention outward to career or community, the introverted intuitive may look around for someone who shares their interests and "understands" them. If the extraverted feeling type cannot get their needs met constructively, they may overindulge in alcohol, a series of flirtations, or impulsive buying sprees.

If the EFJ is the male in the relationship, his caring qualities and ease in expressions of feeling will make him very attractive to members of the opposite sex. Many women are so hungry for an interaction with a male who will talk about something besides sports and politics that they tend to become infatuated with their minister, their doctor, or their therapist, if he is able to talk their language of "feeling." While an INJ female tends to be independent and self-sufficient, jealousy of female reactions to their partners can lead to hurt and resentful feelings.

Some Helpful Hints

If both types are intuitive, each will have considerable knowledge of the other's needs and wants. It is always good to check intuitions out, however and not make assumptions. If one is an ESFJ, this type can complement the intuitive's lack of interest in dealing with the factual world by creating some time and space (often with some humor) to deal with any necessary tasks. The intuitive can offer creative suggestions for some ways that might make those tasks easier. Both types tend to be responsive and responsible, so a division of labor is usually easily attainable.

Extraverted Feeling Types (ESFJ/ENFJ) with Introverted Thinking Types (ISTP/INTP)

When it's working: Although introverted thinking types may not express themselves verbally, if their extraverted feeling type mates can read between the lines, they will be aware of the introverted thinking type's devotion to home and family. Perhaps just because of the introverted thinking type's difficulty in being understood by others or in forming easy relationships, those they do form are of special importance to them.

Although the extraverted feeling type may carry 80 percent of the interaction with their offspring, the introverted thinking type is apt to appreciate rather than sabotage the intimacy that results from that interaction. Having time to devote to their own pursuits (whether to the development of a new theory or the refining of a new technique) is of primary importance to an introverted thinking type. If the extraverted feeling type can function without the kind of attention they might desire, and understand that their mate is not rejecting them or searching for someone new, the relationship can endure.

When it's not working: It's in this couple that the following interaction might take place: EFJ: "Do you still love me? You never tell me you love me anymore." ITP: "Why do I have to tell you that I love you? I married you, didn't I?"

If the extraverted feeling type is insecure in any way as to their desirability as a mate, they are very unlikely to develop much in the way of self-confidence if they are married to an introverted thinking type. ITPs aren't cruel, but they do tend to be out of touch with their own emotions and feeling responses and even more so to those of others. Feelings are a world they neither want to live in nor comprehend. The more the extraverted feeling type pursues their mate for an expression of feeling, the more the introverted thinking type is likely to withdraw—either into books or into sports. This may leave their mate frustrated and resentful, wondering if they're getting any of their needs met at all in this marriage to an alien creature. In fact, both individuals in this pairing are often likely to wonder what attracted them to each other in the first place. The sexual attraction may be the only bond that's left between them.

Some Helpful Hints

If couples in this combination of types are sufficiently mature to appreciate their differences and help each other to develop different aspects of themselves, their relationship can work. What the extraverted feeling type can offer their mate is an ease in dealing with the environment, sensitivity to others, and skills in relating. In return, the introverted thinking type may teach the extraverted feeling type the skills of introspection, the art of concentration, and the value in being self-directed rather than being controlled by others—particularly by people in authority.

Extraverted Sensing Types (ESTP/ESFP) with Introverted Sensing Types (ISTJ/ISFJ)

When it's working: If a couple composed of this pairing of types utilize their individual strengths in a balanced cooperative manner, they will learn from each other, appreciate each other's differences, and value what each has to offer in the relationship.

Financial matters will need to be handled carefully for this pair. The introverted sensing type needs the security of a bank account with savings sufficient to cover any emergencies. The extraverted sensing type needs to be able to satisfy their risk-taking proclivities. An understanding and appreciation of each other's needs can result in the development of a system that works, whether it's separate accounts, allotted percentages of income, or whatever seems fair to both.

The extraverted sensing types can keep their introverted sensing type partners from settling into a rut, which, no matter how comfortable, can end up being boring and depressing to the extraverted sensing type. The introverted sensing types can keep their extraverted sensing type partners from jumping off some cliff without looking to see if there's a safe landing place below. That is, if their differences are understood and valued.

When it's not working: A marriage between an extraverted sensing type and an introverted sensing type can be a disaster if there is not an appreciation of each other's gifts. Each will feel the other is deliberately thwarting them in the pursuit of their goals. Anger, bitterness and resentment can mount on both sides. If you can imagine a marriage between a grasshopper and an ant, you may gain some understanding of what might occur. The ant knows what it has to do, how busy it has to be, how hard it has to work, and wants its partner to pull its share of the load. The grasshopper knows how much fun it is to leap around and have experiences and trust the future to take care of itself—and will want its partner to play along and not worry over everything.

Of course, if the relationship gets too heavy or uncomfortable, the grasshopper (or ESP) is very likely to just hop out of it. Extraverted sensing types, if they are unable to effect compromises, are not likely to remain too long in situations that don't please them. The introverted sensing type, no matter how unhappy, is much less likely to initiate a separation once they've entered a relationship. They'll often keep trying to make it work.

Extraverted sensing types seem less likely than most types to go into therapy. Most do not enjoy the process of introspection, and would simply rather escape into another environment. So, if anyone does ask for counseling, it will probably be the introverted sensing type. Counseling can be effective in helping the introverted sensing type in gaining a larger perspective on the situation and releasing the emotions that have been built up.

Some Helpful Hints

Extraverted sensing types can add the sparkle, zest, and excitement with life that the steady, reliable introverted sensing types often crave. Introverted sensing types can provide the stability that is missing in the lives of many extraverted sensing types. And the children born to this couple can benefit from having one parent who is always there for them and another who provides the fun and unexpected surprises that delight them.

Extraverted Sensing Types (ESTP/ESFP) with Introverted Feeling Types (ISFP/INFP)

When it's working: When these two types become involved with each other, the attraction, especially the sexual attraction, can be very strong. The differences in style may seem puzzling and intriguing, with the depth and inner world of the introverted feeling type being a challenge to the extraverted sensing type. The flair and ease with which the extraverted sensing type handles the outer world can be a source of amazement to the introverted feeling type.

With their children, the extraverted sensing type is likely to create a sense of fun and excitement. Play time is highly valued, and involvement in sports is likely to be encouraged. If there are problems, however, with a child being ill or unhappy, it is more likely the introverted feeling type who will come through and provide the support the child may need.

If the extraverted sensing type tends to experiment with the financial resources the family has available, this will probably affect the introverted feeling type to a lesser degree than it would most other introverts. Money and material possessions generally hold less value for introverted feeling types than for other types. When the extraverted sensing type is successful financially, it frees the introverted feeling type from dealing with having to make ends meet and allows them to pursue their interests in writing, painting, research, or wherever their creativity may lead them.

When it's not working: Sometimes, the differences in style between these two types will lead to intense clashes between the values each lives by. Expediency and idealism make strange bedfellows, and when mutual respect disappears from the relationship, there is not much left to keep it glued together.

There will undoubtedly be more problems for this couple if the male is the introverted feeling type; for, despite the fact that more couples are moving into the partnership mode, males are often still expected to be the primary financial provider. An undiscovered artist or a poorly paid researcher may not fit the stereotype of the male financial provider. Introverted feeling types need support and encouragement more than any other type.

Problems with children for this pairing can also be severe. The extraverted sensing type is more likely than other types to disappear if the going gets tough, for life is supposed to be fun and exciting. While the extraverted sensing type might withdraw physically, the introverted feeling type may withdraw into their own world to avoid dealing with situations they feel are beyond their control. One bad result could be children feeling both physically and emotionally abandoned at the very times when parents are most needed. It might be wise for this combination of types to postpone parenting until some of their own dynamics have been resolved.

Some Helpful Hints

If the nitty-gritty details of everyday life don't interfere in the process, these two have a great deal to learn from each other. The introverted feeling type can help the extraverted sensing type become more self-aware and develop a richness of character rather than coasting on the surface of life. The extraverted sensing type can help the introverted feeling type to see the world and their own strengths more realistically. They can also teach introverted feeling types more effective social skills.

Extraverted Sensing Types (ESTP/ESFP) with Introverted Intuitive Types (INTJ/INFJ)

When it's working: If you want to look at the attraction of opposites, you'll find it in this pairing. Extraverted sensing types are very much "outer" directed. They are always aware of who wants what and why, and their actions tend to be governed by these perceptions. Introverted intuitive types are very much "inner" directed, and are likely to ignore what is going on around them because of the intensity with which they focus on their goals. These styles may complement each other, and indeed each has a lot to learn from the other. However, the pairing is very unusual and there is apparently little to hold such a couple together past the initial dating period. If they do wind up together, adjustments need to be made on both sides but it is more likely to be the extraverted sensing type who adjusts. While an INFJ may "accommodate" somewhat, the INTJ is unlikely to do so.

If the extraverted sensing type reads reserve as a weakness or compliance in any introverted intuitive type, their misperception may lead to a rude awakening. If they understand their mate and value the strengths their mate possesses (despite the differences from their own), they can work to develop a satisfying relationship.

With children, the introverted intuitive type may provide the stability and resourcefulness required. An INFJ especially is likely to be bonded emotionally and psychically with their offspring. While the extraverted sensing type may provide more fun and stimulation, the introverted intuitive type will probably be the primary parent.

When it's not working: When the romantic glow of a fresh relationship is gone, this couple may step back and see each other in the cold hard glare of reality or what is perceived as reality. The introverted intuitive type who values integrity above all else may be seen by their mate as rigid, impractical, eccentric, and from another planet. The extraverted sensing type who values an ability to make things work may be seen by their mate as too ready to let the end justify the means, as manipulative, as flighty, and with no sense of values. Disapproval, lack of respect, and a scornful demeanor never help a relationship survive.

The long range goals and the vision of the future that the introverted intuitive brings to the relationship do not provide much immediate satisfaction for the extraverted sensing type who is much more likely to live in the here and now and want what they want today. The expensive gifts or exciting toys purchased by the extraverted sensing type may be seen as directly sabotaging the future purchase of a home about which the introverted intuitive type has been dreaming. Battles over finances and who is to control the checkbook will undoubtedly play a large role in this couple's life.

Some Helpful Hints

Talking things out and seeking resolutions that will bring at least a moderate degree of satisfaction to each partner will have a large pay-off in the prevention of built-up resentments and hostilities. The finances are best handled by the introverted intuitive type; recreation by the extraverted sensing type. The willingness to let each do what he or she does best will help resolve differences. The introverted intuitive needs to be willing to go along on some "fun" expeditions that may seem like a waste of time, and the extraverted sensing type needs to check in with their partner on large expenditures while still having "play" money.

Extraverted Sensing Types (ESTP/ESFP) with Introverted Thinking Types (ISTP/INTP)

When it's working: This combination of types works best when the introverted thinking type is an ISTP rather than an INTP. An INTP is likely to appear too detached from the real world to either respond to or appeal to the extraverted sensing type. And "logically" (which is how an INTP operates) a relationship with someone so very different in perceptions, style, and values would not make much sense. Some INTPs are environmentalists. This focus on the environment can help the extraverted sensing type bridge the gap if the introverted thinker is also intuitive.

An extraverted sensing type and ISTP approach life as an adventure, with excitement holding a high priority for both. Conventions, conservatism, hide-bound rules will hold little appeal for either, and both will congratulate themselves and each other for not being stuck with someone who would be dull, plodding, and resistant to change.

Children born to this couple will be encouraged to take risks and to live life fully. There will be little negative judgment of academic performance, and encouragement in athletic activities may be given priority over reading or other more academic pursuits. If these children are also SPs, this will work well, for they will be validated for their strengths rather than invalidated for their weaknesses.

When it's not working: When things go awry for this couple, they may find fault with each other, attach blame, and not understand why someone isn't picking up the pieces and bringing order our of chaos.

Household chores and other tasks will be seen as a bore. If the man had a more traditional mother who played a typical housewife role, he may be overly critical of a woman who is not willing to play that same role.

Both may withdraw either physically or emotionally when problems arise, and if there are children there may be little stability in their environment.

Some Helpful Hints

If the introverted thinking type is willing to come out and discover some of life's adventures from another perspective and the extraverted sensing type can sometimes find time for interesting discussions as well as activities, they can share each other's world. Extraverted sensing types are very aware and interested in everything that is happening around them. If the introverted thinking type's interest happens to focus on environmental concerns also, their interests can provide for lively discussions and even accomplishments.

Extraverted Intuitive Types (ENTP/ENFP) with Introverted Sensing Types (ISTJ/ISFJ)

When it's working: If these very different styles can complement each other, this relationship has good potential. The extraverted intuitive can bring excitement and freedom and the introverted sensing type can provide stability and security. Few types can rival the introverted sensing type for dependability and a sensible approach to life. Few types can rival the extraverted intuitive for ease of manner and lively discourse. If one in the couple happens to be F and one is T, they are opposite on every scale. While that can be a challenge, the possibilities to look at the unconscious aspects of self mirrored in the other person and learn from them are readily available right at home. That could be a real asset if looked at in the best way possible.

When it's not working: Chances are the introverted sensing type will want a predictable, traditional lifestyle—good steady job for one or both, dinner at home, enough money to be able to plan and budget—values that the extraverted intuitive can find inhibiting of freedom. The extraverted intuitive may get caught up and forget to call home when expected—a behavior which can cause friction for the couple.

An example from our practice: One of the couples we worked with were definitely in love with one another—but Alice had already made an appointment with a divorce lawyer and Jerry couldn't understand why. Alice (an ISTJ) said she couldn't live with the uncertainties in their marriage. It all boiled down to the fact that Jerry would say he'd be home by eight at the latest—she would hold dinner for him—and he'd finally get home sometimes at midnight. He would claim he was talking with the other junior executives over a couple of drinks and that important decisions would get taken care of during that time. Finally Jerry was able to understand that Alice couldn't handle worrying about where he was after the 8 o'clock deadline. What we finally agreed on was that we would get Jerry a wallet with "Call Alice" engraved on the inside. So if Jerry were to pay a bar bill he would be reminded that Alice was waiting to hear from him. On her part, Alice agreed not to say "Come home right now". Several years have passed and Alice and Jerry have managed to work out differences through using negotiating skills rather than with threats and tantrums, or ignoring one partner's concerns.

Js tend to expect a certain routine to be followed; Ps tend to go with the flow. The introverted sensing type may interpret it as not caring about them if the extraverted intuitive doesn't show up for a dinner prepared for them. The extraverted intuitive may interpret it as controlling that dinnertime seems so inflexible.

Some Helpful Hints

Introverted sensing types want the real world handled; extraverted intuitive types want to experience the world of possibilities. Both needs should be taken care of for this relationship to work well.

Introverted sensing types need to be careful not to seem to make demands which feed into the extraverted intuitive types' natural resistance to any structure they haven't participated in and agreed to follow.

Extraverted intuitive types need to not be seen as elusive and hedonistic to the more dependable introverted sensing types and be willing to participate in some of the more boring duties that are present in any relationship. Extraverted intuitives will respond better if it can be fun rather than just a chore—so put the music on, laugh and talk together and get the work done. It doesn't always have to be serious.

Extraverted Intuitive Types (ENTP/ENFP)
with Introverted Feeling Types (ISFP/INFP)

When it's working: The sensitivity possible in this relationship can be outstanding. The possibilities for following a dream of self-fulfillment also exist here. Neither type is bound by convention or tradition. If both partners are NF, they can have a love that would rival that of a romantic movie's hero and heroine. When both types are feeling types, the shared experience of feeling values can keep the relationship alive and well. Even though the ENTP may not share a feeling orientation with their partner, they still need open expression in an intimate relationship since they don't often allow themselves to be vulnerable in other situations. An active social life and a meaningful personal life will characterize this relationship when it's working.

When it's not working: The extraverted intuitive may feel he or she is coming home to someone who doesn't understand them or appreciate them if they get little or no response. The introverted feeling type may give up trying to interact much with the extraverted intuitive type if their moods seem to be unpredictable. NFs typically want harmony and both may try to avoid unpleasantness until it gets almost too big to handle. The ENTP in this group is more likely to confront earlier which may also be alienating if it is not done in a sensitive way for the introverted feeling type. Distance, less talk, and resentful moods can characterize this relationship when it's not working, although the introverted feeling type can sometimes be explosive as well.

Some Helpful Hints

Both need to pay enough attention to the other. The extraverted intuitive type can get caught up in the outer world and the introverted feeling type in their own pursuits. Mundane tasks need to be divided and handled when the person is ready, not on any schedule. Criticism needs to be constructive and kept to a minimum. Manifesting at least part of their dreams, while managing the world well enough will keep them feeling good about each other. The creative potential that exists is also outstanding in this relationship. If the extraverted intuitive can help translate the introverted feeling type's ideals into reality, it can be fulfilling for both. Extraverted intuitives tend to want to be all things to all people since their intuition is directed outwardly. Introverted feeling types tend to want their inner ideals accepted and valued by the outer world, but sometimes have difficulty in finding a means to express those ideals that brings the results they hope to achieve.

Extraverted Intuitive Types (ENTP/ENFP) with Introverted Intuitive Types (INTJ/INFJ)

When it's working: Theoretically at least, all the knowledge and possibilities in the universe are available to this couple. The extraverted intuitive type focuses on the outer world and the introverted intuitive type on the inner world. The combination of their insights could be awesome. What to do with all those insights could be a problem although the excitement and depth possible here may manifest in a very romantic way. Intuitives tend to be very aware of relationship "atmosphere", so sensitivity to each other is another plus in this relationship. Introverted intuitives can get too caught up in being responsible. A sensitive partner can monitor that and help out. Extraverted intuitives can spread themselves too thin—again a sensitive partner is a wonderful person to come home to and rest.

When it's not working: If both types get caught up and busy in handling the world, the sensitivity may be more for themselves than each other. The introverted intuitive may resent the time and energy spent outside the relationship, especially if it is paired with not being responsible at home. The more the extraverted intuitive picks up the resentment or lack of warmth from their partner, the more they may stay away from home, thus aggravating the whole syndrome. They may also look for a friend outside to share things with, which would feel like a violation to the introverted intuitive. The need for good energy to keep the engine running is important for the extraverted intuitive. The need for loving involvement in depth from one person is important for the introverted intuitive.

Some Helpful Hints

Each needs to use their expanded awareness to take care of the other's needs in the way that the other person needs to receive it. The introverted intuitive may simply need more help with handling some of the responsibilities that sometimes weigh so heavily on them and they find difficult to put down. The extraverted intuitive may simply need a good experience and interaction which allows them the energy to respond to some of the more routine needs of the relationship. If both remember that what we give is usually what we want back in a relationship, not necessarily what comes naturally to the other person, it will help. Intuitives have more natural ability to see the other side than most other types. An introverted intuitive at least sometimes needs a responsible partner, which an extraverted intuitive has difficulty being unless it is in their own time and their own way. An extraverted intuitive needs a good experience of the relationship, which the introverted intuitive has difficulty providing if they are feeling resentful about responsibilities. They both need to use their creativity and good will to get out of any stalemate. Otherwise the extraverted intuitive may escape; the introverted intuitive may be alienated and sulk alone.

Extraverted Intuitive Types (ENTP/ENFP) with Introverted Thinking Types (ISTP/INTP)

When it's working: If the types with thinking in this combination become partners, there can be a great deal of understanding and even a similar though different pursuit of each one's own unique interests while maintaining the relationship. If one in the couple has thinking and one has feeling as a preference, the relationship can be enhanced by offering a different perspective on values (F) and concepts (T). In the couples we counsel, types with thinking as one preference and types with feeling as one preference do tend to pair up. Sharing the different insights or experiences gained through pursuing their individual interests can add sparkle to the relationship. The extraverted intuitive can be too wordy and the introverted thinking type too terse. Patience for the manner of expression and appreciation of the content makes for a more stimulating dialogue without judgment of style.

When it's not working: The extraverted intuitive who likes to be all things to all people may seek more excitement and fun than the introverted thinking type who by nature is thoughtful and into their own way of looking at things. Communication can become frustrating or break down. The people-contact need of the extravert and the alone-time need of the introvert can also cause conflicts in how time and energy are expended. Many ISTPs and INTPs are very good with computers and may want to spend a lot of time in their own "virtual reality" world. Both types tend to be original and creative and this aspect of their characters needs to be appreciated rather than criticized because "you need to be more like me."

Some Helpful Hints

New and creative ideas will always intrigue the extraverted intuitive as will new ways of saying things. If the introverted thinking type is willing to share more of their private world, communication will be better. Both types would rather do their own thing their own way than respond to any one else's rules or methods. It is important for each to give the other room to be the way they are and appreciate the positive aspects of a different style. The more social extraverted intuitive can bring a more lively involvement in life and the thoughtful introverted thinking type can help find ways to "program" some of the more ordinary details to help both be free to do their individual things. The introverted thinking type is great at devising a system. The extraverted intuitive is great at generating enthusiasm. That combination has the possibility of making great things happen.

Resources

Grant, W. Harold, Magdala Thompson, and Thomas Clarke, *From Image to Likeness: A Jungian Path In the Gospel Journey.*
Kroeger, Otto and Janet Thuesen, *16 Ways To Love Your Lover.*
Kummerow, Jean. *Verifying Your Type Preferences.*
Lawrence, Gordon, *People Types and Tiger Stripes.*

CHAPTER VII

A Closer Look at
Common Conflict Areas

"The artful denial of a problem will not produce conviction;
on the contrary, a wider and higher consciousness is called for
to give us the certainty and clarity we need."
—C. G. Jung,
Modern Man in Search of a Soul, p. 97

Our clinical population is from Hawaii where we have been in practice for over 25 years. Hawaii is both liberal and conservative. On one side it was the first state to pass the equal rights amendment. On the other side, many residents have traditional values, although most women in the State work. Since we have many immigrants from Asia, the Pacific Islands and the Philippines, we have many men who expect to be "head of the household." Some expect to be able to define the woman's role as is done in their native countries. Transitions are currently in process, however.

Many psychologists, sociologists, and anthropologists have studied both successful and unsuccessful relationships in an attempt to predict the possibility of two people living "happily ever after." Similarity of cultural variables such as race, religion, ethnic origin, socioeconomic class, and age provide a less stressful background against which to play out intimate interactions, but in themselves provide no guarantee that a relationship will last. Most research looks at being alike or different in terms of marriage, but the concepts fit relationships in general—between men and women, or couples that are both men or both women. Though we may give examples of male-female relationships our experience is that type concepts apply to lesbian and gay couples also.

We have found that it is possible to look at relatively good relationships and to identify areas in which conflicts are likely to occur. Couples in these relationships may be similar in terms of cultural variables. There are no indications of wife or child abuse, no problem of alcohol or drug addiction, no incest, no involvement in criminal activities. These apparent similarities are not enough to keep a relationship from breaking up.

There are certain areas of potential conflict which can make or break the relationship. These areas, for any two people living together in an intimate relationship, often fall into the following twelve categories: (1) Communication, (2) Money, (3) Sex and Affection, (4) Values, (5) Interests, (6) Recreation, (7) Decision-making, (8) Time and Responsibility, (9) Chores, (10) Children, (11) In-laws, and (12) Friends.

We would like to take a closer look at these areas with you, see how they may relate to the interaction of your partner's type with your own, and suggest some do's and don't's for resolution of some of the problems you may be having. Also included are some charts on stress, love preferences for the types, descriptions of how they fight, and other perspectives on possibilities for interaction.

Power Factors in Conflicts

The first three areas of potential conflict (Communication, Money, and Sex) are often the arena in which needs for power and control are played out. The struggle may be obvious or subtle, conscious or unconscious. If there are any problems in almost any other area of your relationship, those problems will probably also manifest here. In other words, how we spend our money, when and how we "make love," and whose ideas prevail after a discussion are important factors in establishing some kind of equity or balance in the relationship. If one person feels she or he must go along with the other and there is no real choice, anger and resentment start to build up whether it is expressed or not. On the other hand, if each individual can trust that the decisions are mutual and in both people's best interests, the relationship is strengthened and enhanced.

Communication

Communication—the act of expressing and/or listening—may be verbal or non-verbal. Sometimes a look or gesture will have more meaning than the words spoken. A gentle hand on the shoulder, a look that says "I'm really glad to see you," a wink and a smile can brighten a dull day for either partner. These days, just as in the past, women tend to voice dissatisfaction with the quality and quantity of communication to a much greater degree than do men. Relationship counseling is often instigated by the woman in an attempt to get her needs in this area met.

Satisfying communication is essential to a relationship. Almost everyone who comes for relationship counseling starts out defining the problem in terms of communication. The specifics of this are important and often get into type behavior. Many people resist being specific, but it is necessary for understanding especially where types differ. "What does she say that makes you angry?" "How do you feel controlled by his moods?" The effects of being extraverted or introverted seem to have more impact on communication problems than do the other preferences. These problems seem to intensify when the woman is the extravert and the man the introvert. If you will remember that extraverts need to interact or dialogue with others in order to clarify their thoughts or feelings and that introverts need to process internally prior to dialoguing, you can understand why their needs might be in conflict. Added to this is the fact that extraverts are energized by interaction, and introverts are often drained.

If you have an introverted partner out spending energy in interactions on the job and an extraverted partner at home bursting with energy and starved for adult conversation, you can see why their encounter at the front door when they meet in the evening might be less than satisfying for both.

One of our extraverted clients, thoroughly frustrated with her introverted thinking partner, reported:

> He doesn't say things that need to be said, how he feels about the situation, how he feels about me. As an example, we've talked quite a bit recently—or I have—about my having too much of the burden of housework, child care, etc. In your office he said that he felt badly about this. He never said that to me. His response to things that upset me is often so blah that sometimes I find myself yelling just to get through to him. If I try to bring up problems he either gets preoccupied with TV or a book, or interrupts with superficial solutions.

Another extraverted woman reported:

He doesn't want to hear anything bad, sad, or upsetting if it concerns me. So I have not been relating my innermost thoughts and fears to him—and this is not how I expected marriage to be.

Introverts also voice complaints, as one man reported:

I always felt I did 90 percent of the listening and that what I had to say was of marginal importance. She just gets frustrated when I have difficulty articulating what's bothering me and walks away.

Perhaps an incident from my own marriage (Ruth) will demonstrate what happens when needs are in conflict. Some years ago, my husband and I were awakened by the police telling us that our daughter had been in an accident and that she was being taken to a hospital. On the drive to the hospital, my extraverted husband needed to talk to handle his anxiety. I could not talk. I needed my energy to handle my feelings and get them under control so I could be calm and supportive for my daughter when we arrived at the hospital.

Neither of us was bad or wrong, but I was unable to give him the conversation he needed to handle his feelings, and he was unable to give me the quiet I needed to handle my feelings.

The difference between the ways sensing and intuitive types see a situation leads many couples to talk past each other. If one partner wants to talk about what can be and the other confronts them with "the facts," the first partner may get very frustrated. On the other hand, if the first partner is ignoring the facts in favor of their dream the other partner may get equally frustrated. Why discuss buying a house if we have no money? Sensing types may bore intuitive types with details. Intuitives may just start talking in the middle of things and not be clear to sensing types.

Thinking-feeling differences in making judgments can be mutually helpful or can lead to conflicts. Thinking men often express dissatisfaction about communications with feeling women: "She's impossible to reason with. Her logic is non-existent on most topics, regardless of the critical nature of the topic." The woman in this situation was equally frustrated: "He makes me feel backed up against the wall—like we're playing some game and I don't know the rules. He makes me feel inadequate and then I get furious with him."

Feeling type women can infuriate thinking type men, especially intuitive feeling type women who believe "If you really loved me you would know how I feel." They are not always willing to tell the man how they feel since "he should already know." A thinking type man has difficulty unlocking his own feelings let alone those of his partner, even if the effort is made.

An ENTP, voicing discouragement with an introverted feeling partner, stated: "If I say something my partner disagrees with, she turns away completely and will not speak to me at all—about anything—sometimes for days. So we almost never get anything important resolved."

Judging types can seem pushy and demanding in their need for closure. Perceiving types can bring decisions up again after their partners thought it was settled. "I thought we decided we were taking our vacation at the beach this year." This statement could be met with "I know, but I think I'd really rather go camping or hiking."

If these problems seem similar to some of the ones you're experiencing in your own relationship, here are some practical solutions that we've found to be effective in keeping communication open and healthy.

Don'ts

1. Don't bring up controversial issues at a busy time. Hold them for weekend or after-dinner discussions when you can give them time and attention without being pressured.
2. Don't use information that's been shared earlier against your partner in an argument. It's one sure way to destroy trust.
3. Don't rush to fill in the gaps if you're waiting for a response from an introverted partner. A few moments of silence can even be useful.
4. Don't talk "over" or louder than the other person, especially when you disagree. Wait your turn or say, "I need my turn now."
5. Don't make judgments until you have heard your partner. It's easy to assume incorrectly that you know what they're going to say.

Do's

1. Wait awhile to communicate with an introverted partner when he/she walks in the door after a day at work. Give introverts a chance to regroup their energies by soaking in a tub, reading their newspapers, watching TV, or whatever else gives them an opportunity to go "inside" and process their day. Depending on the stress of the day, anywhere from twenty minutes to an hour should prepare them to share with you—and it will be better quality sharing.
2. Those of you who are introverts need to learn to share with your partner. In a partnership both people need to be informed of at least the important events and also need a personal information update periodically.
3. Schedule time for sharing if you can. A long leisurely walk after dinner (the dishes can wait till you get home) without the interruptions of the telephone, TV, or children can provide the appropriate structure and atmosphere for continuing dialogues.
4. Extraverts, many of whom love to talk, need to remember to leave a safe opening in the conversation for an introverted partner to respond. Introverts will usually talk if they feel comfortable. If introverts perceive they are in a conflict situation they may say nothing or leave as soon as possible.
5. Learn to speak the other person's type "language" just a little to appreciate their point of view better and to be more patient with them.

Before engaging in too serious a conversation with your partner or mate, you might take a moment to facilitate the process.

When you want to communicate with —

Extraverts, because of all the competing outer world things to attend to,
Say: May I have your attention now, or if not, when?

Introverts, because of all the competing inner world things to attend to,
Say: Are you available for what I want to talk about?

Sensing types, because they prefer to focus on tangibles,
Say: Can we be creative about this?

Intuitives, because they prefer to focus on intangibles,
Say: Do you have a reality base for what you're saying?

Thinking types, because they prefer to stay somewhat detached,
Say: This is something very important to me. I need you to understand, not solve.

Feeling types, because they prefer to get quite involved,
Say: Take a moment to consider this point of view before you respond.

Judging types, because they want to know what the plan is,
Say: Please keep an open mind while I explore options with you.

Perceptive types, because they want to have it all,
Say: Tell me what's most important to you.

Resources

Kummerow, Jean, *Talking in Type*.
Lawrence, Gordon, *Communication Patterns*.

Finances

The power conflicts in this area generally relate to the earning, management, and distribution of income. It wasn't so long ago that a married woman who worked could be an embarrassment to her husband as if he could not support her. Now, we know of no one who doesn't want her/his partner to work and earn money.

It is almost an economic necessity for both partners to work. Having children is often worked in with a career, sometimes with only six weeks off before returning to work. Women today know their freedom is tied in with economic independence. Relationships may not last "til death do us part," even though we still may say those words.

Women who are self-supporting are being assertive and are demanding equity in economic decisions. These societal changes can also create more open conflicts than when one partner has had total say and could just dole out an "allowance" for the other to manage. The division of responsibility also has to be redefined with women working. Some men may still believe they are better with money decisions and be reluctant to pick up household responsibilities. Women may still feel responsible for the home, but resent that some men may think their responsibility ends when they enter "their castle." Remember: "Where love rules, there is no will to power." We can negotiate for what we want out of love and not power or control needs. We need to check our own motivations.

Type differences also contribute to power struggles over family finances. Sensing-judging mates are likely to hold conservative values where money is concerned—to invest carefully, to want to own a home, to have an annuity, to start a fund for a child's education. A sensing-perceiving partner may be more willing to take risks with money, not to want to be tied down to a job or community through ownership of a home. One ESFP woman reported in a counseling session that she felt controlled by her ESTJ partner who invariably tried to talk her out of spending. "I often agree that what I want isn't necessary, but then I feel angry and resentful."

Differences in type also produce other differences in beliefs about how money should be spent. An introverted feeling type (INFP) wistfully reported: "I'd much rather have had a romantic vacation—even a weekend—than the dishwasher my (ISTJ) partner bought me!"

Some needs are real for each type. Judging types do need to feel secure about money. They may just want a savings account. Perceiving types do need to feel somewhat free to spend. They may want a vacation account. Extraverted perceiving types may take risks that make introverted judging types anxious. They may like to gamble occasionally. Each type needs to get as many needs met as possible without jeopardizing the partner's mental health. Some types can pull off a big gamble; others are better savers. Know your capabilities and limitations as well as those of your partner and set up your finances accordingly.

The probability is that you are different in type from your partner. If you are, especially on the sensing-intuitive or judging-perceiving preferences, we recommend the following actions:

Don'ts

1. Don't make each other account for every penny.
2. Don't expect to continue to use your money any way you choose. In a relationship, how you spend your money has an impact on your partner.
3. Don't use credit cards (except for gas) if one of you is a compulsive or impulsive spender.
4. Don't plan only for the present or the future; both need to be considered.

Do's

1. Set up triple checking accounts (yours, mine, and ours) with either a small percentage of each salary—if salaries are fairly equitable—or matched amounts going into the individual accounts. Neither partner should have to account to the other for expenditures out of the individual account, so make sure you're comfortable with the arrangement before you begin.

2. Another alternative is to pool your funds, but consult with each other to reach agreements before expensive items are purchased when shopping alone. Use your own situation to decide the cutoff point: $200, $500, $1000, etc.

3. If one of you is not a wage earner (returning to school, having a baby, etc.), discuss what you are contributing (whether in the present or in the future) until both of you are satisfied that this is a valuable contribution. Without sufficient exploration, discussion, and agreement, both of you may feel used and build up anger or resentment for the future. "You never contributed anything—it was all my hard work and money" or "I gave up my career to have your baby" are common complaints.

4. If one of you has a judging preference and the other a perceiving preference, consider letting the judging one keep the joint checkbook or you may both wind up frustrated.

5. Allow for the fun of spontaneous spending for special things as well as the need for careful bookkeeping.

If one partner is experiencing prolonged or extreme stress, it puts a strain on the relationship. When both people are needy at the same time, the relationship may be in trouble. If one partner loses a parent, the other a job, neither may have much to give each other. Just an awareness of the other's struggle gives some support. Here are some examples of the support your partner may be able to offer.

Type	Help offered to cope with stress
Extraverted Thinking Types (ESTJ, ENTJ)	A natural look at the over-all picture. A description of strategies that may help you to reduce the stress.
Introverted Thinking Types (ISTP, INTP)	You'll get a deep perceptive analysis of the situation that is providing the stress, and solutions for dealing with it that *you* will have to follow through on.
Extraverted Feeling Types (ESFJ, ENFJ)	Sincere caring and support and suggestions on how to deal with some of the people involved in the situation.
Introverted Feeling Types (ISFP, INFP)	Awareness of the depth of their feeling for you. They may also use their creativity to help you see the situation in a lighter view.
Extraverted Sensing Types (ESTP, ESFP)	A fresh awareness of the situation which may help you to develop your own productive insights. An example of how not to stay "caught" in a stressful, non-productive situation.
Introverted Sensing Types (ISTJ, ISFJ)	An awareness that your mate is going to stand by you through this stressful time.
Extraverted Intuitive Types (ENTP, ENFP)	Imaginative, creative problem-solving. Wisdom and insights that may shake you loose.
Introverted Intuitive Types (INTJ, INFJ)	An insightful look at the problem and possibly your own contribution to it.

Sex and Affection

Power issues can affect sexual attitudes and behaviors. Researchers have probably paid more attention to the sexual aspect of relationships than to any other source of marital difficulties. From the extensive research of Kinsey (1948, 1953) and Masters and Johnson (1970) to the popularity of how-to-do-it books and other explicit publications, the focus, at least in America, has been on the pleasures of sex. The underlying assumption seems to be that this could make or break a relationship.

Many men used to want to be the ones who pursued, aggressively seeking affection and sex. Sexual harassment issues have made some men much more cautious in seeking relationships. The current sexual power struggle has changed, and masculine and feminine roles are no longer so clearly defined. Some men want women to initiate and some women are willing to do so. AIDS and HIV have also increased caution with both sexes. "No glove, no love" has become a common saying among single women. Both partners seem to expect someone experienced and talented in love-making rather than a virgin.

In our clinical practice, we hear women as well as men express resentment because their partner is "just not interested" in sex. One EFJ wife, concerned about her relationship with her ITP husband, indicated that: "I would be willing to settle for just 20 to 30 minutes a week for being intimate in bed." Her husband's response was: "If I gave you that, pretty soon you'll want an hour, then two or three hours a week. You're just insatiable."

Many of the women in our practice complain that their partners don't spend enough time talking to them, or aren't willing to discuss their feelings. Many of the men in our practice are more likely to express dissatisfaction with their mates in the sexual arena: "She's always too tired"; "She doesn't understand how hard I work and how tired I am"; "She never wants to try anything new"; "She's always reading books and coming up with some crazy experiments" are some of the most common complaints. Somehow many men seem to focus on this aspect of the relationship and seem to have a strong reaction to it.

During the past twenty-five years, we have seen increasing numbers of women with preferences for extraversion and thinking in our practice, which may represent increasing numbers in our culture. If more and more women can be classified as an "Executive" type (ETJ), and are increasingly found in executive careers, it is important to consider the effects of these changes on the sexual relationship. Executives and "executive" types are likely to be assertive, perhaps even aggressive, in their interactions. Finances and sex are two areas where control issues are easily seen. A woman who is used to being an executive at the office may have to shift gears to share power in these arenas at home. The same is true for men. More women executives may make this struggle more pervasive.

Similarities and/or differences on the other MBTI preferences also play a part in what occurs sexually between partners. Sensing types are generally more likely to be in touch with their sensuality; intuitives are more likely to have romantic fantasies and to respond if there is an element of romance introduced into the physical aspects of sexual intercourse.

Types with intuition and feeling (NFs), whether introvert or extravert, judging or perceiving, often make love a priority. Good feelings, given and received may be more important to them than for other types. One SJ man continually complained that his wife was "never interested." After we learned in our sessions that receiving a bouquet of fresh-cut flowers could be almost guaranteed to turn her on, we communicated that to her husband. Unfortunately, this very practical man saw bouquets as "impractical" and continued to bring her potted plants as an expression of his affection.

Sexual relationships outside the primary relationship can cause major reactions and emotions. Differences between judging types and perceiving types may play a role in both behavior and in attitudes. One young J husband reported that he didn't feel right about extra-marital affairs. "It seems to me that pursuing affairs indicates a lack of commitment which two people make with each other. I would like to see us make an honest effort to fulfill each other's needs." One example of a newly-married ESP woman expressed a different point of view:

> We have a difference of opinion in that extra-marital affairs are okay with me as long as they don't interfere with our relationship. Sexual intimacy has greater significance for him. Of course, even if he decided extra-marital relationships were okay for both of us, we're not sure we'd act on it. We realize if we did, a lot of working things out would be necessary.

Judging types, as well as perceiving types can become involved outside of the relationship. One ESTJ thought he was "entitled"—after all he had "made it" in the world. An ENTJ found someone who seemed to make up for everything she wasn't getting from a late-working partner.

The AIDs epidemic is affecting attitudes towards sexual acting-out for partners. The life-or-death aspect of the disease you may contract yourself or bring home to an unsuspecting partner is creating more frank discussions about sex. The fear of moving back into a social scene with such attendant danger can create more pressure for couples to work on their relationships. There is much more caution about sexual involvement. Most people want monogamy whether they are willing to give it or not.

If you and your partner are experiencing problems or lack of satisfaction in the sexual aspect of your relationship, we offer the following recommendations as possible solutions:

Don'ts

1. If your mate is not responding sexually because of stress, illness, or anxiety, don't rush into another relationship to prove you're still desirable.
2. Don't be angry or critical and then expect your partner to feel loving and responsive sexually. You may feel better; your partner won't.
3. Don't be in a hurry. Some of the greatest intimate moments can occur with the sharing of thoughts and feelings during and following sexual intimacy.
4. Don't get into acting out your partner's fantasies unless that fits your fantasy also. Rather than helping, this can lead to repressed anger and alienation.
5. Don't have too many explicit demands about performances. Where trust, love, and good will prevail, the intimacy can be meaningful, even if not just like the movies or the story books.

Do's

1. Once a month if you can afford it—every three months, even if you can't—hire a baby-sitter if necessary and get away *alone* to a really nice hotel, a cabin in the mountains, or whatever kind of place you both would really enjoy. Get reacquainted with the person you chose to marry. Go dancing if that's what you used to like. Have a bottle of champagne and room service, relax and enjoy each other.
2. Be aware that when there are difficulties in other aspects of your relationship, these difficulties are likely to show up in bed. Take a hard look at the relationship, possibly with the help of an experienced counselor.
3. Be aware that needs can differ, which doesn't make one right, the other wrong. Look for mutually satisfying solutions, even trade-offs if that will work for you. For example: if massaging your partner's feet is relaxing and helps your partner open up sexually, do it. If staying in shape will make you more sexually appealing to your partner, work out.
4. Remember that passion does not always stay at a high peak in even the most ideal relationship. Stress, illness, and anxiety will all affect performance in bed temporarily. Some types may want sex as a comfort or to reduce tension. Decide for yourself if that is O.K. for you also. But, communicate about it!
5. There are many attitudes about sex. It is for procreation, for closeness, for fun, for relaxation, for relieving tension. Find a common bond which includes both individuals' needs if possible.

LOVE PREFERENCES

Knowing the possible effects of each preference in intimate situations may help you avoid some of the problems you might encounter and even allow you to be very sensitive to your partner's needs and desires as well as your own. The following chart provides some of the guidelines to help answer the question "How do I love thee?" when it applies to your mate. Pick out the ones that seem to fit for you and your mate.

Effects of Each Preference in Love Situations

Extraverts	Introverts
Want to be active	Want to be relaxed
Like to be challenged	Want to feel safe
Are willing to initiate	Do not like to initiate
Want variety	Want depth
May invade another's space	May withdraw too far
Have difficulty holding back	Have difficulty freeing up
Are active	Are focused
Like the excitement of a group	Prefer to be alone with the loved one

Sensing Types	Intuitive Types
Want sensual pleasure	Want the right atmosphere
Seek new experiences	Have implicit expectations
Look for different methods	Look for new possibilities
Provide sensory stimulation	Are imaginative
Want sexual contact, then maybe spiritual	Want spiritual contact, then maybe sexual

Thinking Types	Feeling Types
Want to touch intellectually	Want to touch emotionally
Want strategies for successful lovemaking	Want romantic interactions
Want respect	Want expressions of love
Tend to analyze the problem	Tend to be responsive to the partner
Ask their mate to be rational in a crisis	Ask their mate to be understanding in a crisis

Judging Types	Perceiving Types
Want to have commitment	Want to retain freedom
Want continuity and acceptance	Want to go with the flow
Will not respond if certain structures are violated	Will not respond if they feel trapped
Want sex in ways they have had it before	Want to experiment with sex

Internal Factors in Conflicts

The next three areas of conflict which tend to bring couples in for counseling are differences in Values, Interests, and Recreation. Since these all originate from within an individual, we consider them "internal" factors. Mutual respect and accommodation of each other in these areas is more functional in the long range than trying to have it your way in the short range.

Values

Differences in values are often due to difference in type, but also are greatly influenced by parental standards, by education, and by experiences in growing up. It is really unfortunate that some couples never get around to making their values explicit until after the marriage ceremony, or sometimes not until after children are born. How much time and money are allocated for play? Do we want to have children? Do we want to have a stable environment for ourselves and our family or have many new experiences and locations? Is it O.K. to take turns going to school and not working? How much money do I have to make to keep some kind of economic balance in the relationship? Is that even necessary...? These are just some of the questions it might be good to discuss or know about each other before getting too involved.

The more values differ, the more difficult it is likely to be for the partners to negotiate successful resolutions of the problems that will occur. Negotiating values takes mutual respect, not believing there is one right way. Individuals who prefer feeling to thinking often have strong values about people and wanting to do things that will make people happy. One young couple in therapy expressed resentment toward each other because she (an IFP) wanted to allow funds in a very tight budget for buying gifts for family and friends. Her partner, an ISJ with a preference for thinking believed every available penny should go towards the house they were planning to build, and that friends and family could go on hold for several years.

Other ways type may impact on values include:

Extraverts are often more aware of, and responsive to, current trends. Introverts may need what they consider a "better idea" in order to change. They may believe some trends are fads and political correctness can be superficial. Sensing types value common sense, methodical, and incremental change— not leaping into a new concept and welcoming it as intuitives may want to do. Common sense needs may play out as mundane for the intuitive partner who may not share them.

Realism, incremental change, and attention to what is happening NOW are values for sensing types. Vision, imagination, and FUTURE considerations are values for intuitive types.

Thinking types want objectivity and fairness, while feeling types value personal concern, care for people and for the environment.

Judging types like order, planning and predictability while perceiving types want discovery, openness, and flexibility.

Independent of type, similarities or differences in values around food, smoking, alcohol and drugs can also affect a relationship positively or negatively. Everyone would like a healthy partner.

When there are differences in values, we recommend:

Don'ts

1. Don't ask your friends or relatives for opinions. Friends and family will probably have similar experiences and attitudes to yours and will not be able to bring perspective to the situation.
2. Don't be closed and judgmental. Try to see the world through your partner's eyes and try to find something valuable in his or her position.
3. Don't marry someone who holds values very different from yours if you expect them to change after marriage. We have seen relationships break up in which one person wanted children and the other didn't.

Do's

1. Discuss differences in values with an experienced counselor if you discover they are causing problems in the relationship. Values are so close to a person's core that it is extremely difficult to be objective about them. Don't let problems build up. Solve them early.
2. See if you can identify the origin of your own and your partner's values. Sometimes just learning more about the roots of values will make you more able to accept differences in significant others.
3. See if you are open to a different point of view or if there are some things that can't be negotiated.
4. Be explicit if you know up front that you hold a value you cannot change and still preserve your integrity as a person.

A Closer Look at Common Conflict Areas

Interests

Another internal factor in conflicts can be interests. Unlike couples with differing values, those with differing interests can often create satisfying relationships, particularly if both believe that "you don't have to be glued to each other to belong to each other."

When we work with couples with very disparate interests (he loves tennis and fishing, she enjoys the theater and bridge), we will often review with them the activities they participated in during their courtship. Unless there was a great deal of pretense during that time, it is generally possible to uncover some common interests. Of course, if he pretended to enjoy golf to be with her and she pinched herself to keep awake at operas to be with him, we may have to look for new areas of common interest.

Individuals with a preferred sensing function do often tend to share more similar interests—perhaps in nature or sports—and tend to maintain those interests over time. Extraverted sensing types especially like activities and feel maximally alive when "doing" something, especially an activity they enjoy doing.

We all have all preferences at some level, conscious or unconscious. A partner with opposite preferences can open doors to experiences we would not have sought out for ourselves. One person might be surprised that walking can be a joy if it is in a certain place, at a certain time or with a certain person. Someone else might be surprised that ballet can be enchanting and beautiful, and the talent and training it requires can be appreciated. It can make for a richer life to stretch yourself in ways you never imagined until you met your partner.

Extraverts like to be active and going somewhere—not just "sitting around." Introverts like time to reflect or meditate, not always having to be "doing something."

Sensing types may like a great variety of sensory experiences from canoeing to dancing to a special rhythm. Intuitive types like to entertain the possibilities available, perhaps put themselves in each possibility in their imagination and choose one to look forward to in the near future.

Thinking types may enjoy a good game of chess or bridge, a fencing match, literally or figuratively, a battle of "wits." Feeling types may prefer intimate, comfortable contact without having to think about anything, but simply to get that loving feeling.

Judging types may like to know what the plans are, feel secure that appropriate arrangements have been made, put important things first, and try to balance both partners' needs. Perceiving types may prefer spontaneous responses to the environment and people who leave them maximally free to pursue whatever is of interest at the moment.

If this seems to be a problem area for you, we recommend:

Don'ts

1. Don't insist that your partner give up a strong, long-standing interest for the sake of the relationship. You will only breed resentment in your partner and the relationship may feel like a prison to them. If the activity is dangerous, share your concerns and ask them to be careful. If the activity is too time-consuming, ask them to monitor themselves so they provide equal quality time for the relationship.
2. Don't complain and nag during the hours you have together. Use that energy instead to make yourself a more interesting individual.
3. Don't go deeply into an expensive interest that causes financial problems, unless you both agree that it will be worth the investment.
4. Don't be so conservative that it is never possible to use some funds occasionally on an interest that does not pay off. Both partners should have this option.

Do's

1. Put some energy into finding out more about your partner's interests. Sometimes just having more information, like really understanding all the rules about a football game, can make it more interesting for you.
2. See if you can develop a new interest that both of you are beginners at: take a photography class, join a little theater group, take up golf, or help someone with their political campaign. If you live in a college town, there are often a variety of continuing education classes, credit or no-credit, that can stimulate new growth for both of you. Volunteer work with hospitals, environmental groups or other such activities can add a new dimension.
3. If you have young children, consider taking parent-effectiveness training, joining the PTA, etc. Children may already be a shared mutual interest and discussions with other parents can be helpful.

A Closer Look at Common Conflict Areas

Recreation

A third internal factor in relationships is recreation. Interests and recreational activities do overlap, of course, because most people take part in recreational pursuits that satisfy their interests. If you are having problems in this area, you might want to look at yourselves on the preference of introversion-extraversion and see if differences there are contributing to the problem.

Extraverts, in general, have a higher energy level, and will probably want to be out and about doing many activities, usually with someone. If both of you are extraverts, you may both be getting a lot of satisfaction in this area of your relationship. If both of you are introverts, you may both be enjoying spending recreational time just with each other—reading, going to movies, taking long walks together. However, one complaint we do often hear from pairs of introverts is that neither one of them initiates any new activity, and at the end of a long weekend both feel restless and that the weekend was "wasted" reading the newspapers, watching TV, or maybe not even getting dressed.

If you two are different on the extraversion-introversion preference, more adjustments and compromises may be called for. This difference can also be an asset—since the extravert can pull the introvert into fascinating experiences they might never experience otherwise and the introvert can encourage intimate times alone which the extravert might not otherwise experience. Sharing and using the differences constructively helps build a good relationship.

Sensing types are more likely to want recreation that is a new experience, and intuitive types are more likely to prefer recreation that has a creative edge, even if it encompasses the experiential. Being willing to go into the other person's world to some extent can help each of you grow. An intuitive might attend a poetry reading; a sensing type might prefer a tennis match. Why not stretch a little and find out what your partner values in the experience you wouldn't normally choose?

A battle of wits is almost always fun for thinking types; being appreciated is always great for feeling types. If you play games, the thinking type may prefer to win. The feeling type may just want to be appreciated and included. Thinking types like appreciation also, but are more willing to actively compete.

If some kind of performance is entailed in the recreation, how important is it to meet some standard or simply to participate? Can "constructive criticism" be framed as positive suggestions, rather than what is wrong? Instead of "You're not doing it right", use "It might work better if you...."

Judging types may prefer a regular or scheduled time to do something recreational and look forward to it. Perceiving types may prefer to decide on the spur of the moment what to do. Each partner needs to be willing to shift occasionally into the other's style and plan or just go for it. Neither partner should call the shots all the time.

If you're experiencing problems in this area, we recommend:

Don'ts

1. Don't set up too busy a recreation schedule on work days, if you have found it gets in the way of your relationship. If one of you is tired or has had a bad day at work, you won't be much fun to be with. Sometimes, though, it can help change a bad day if the recreation is relaxing or enjoyable.
2. Don't spoil your partner's fun if your mate has chosen an activity you're not that crazy about. If you were doing the activity with a stranger, you'd probably at least be polite and pretend you were having a good time. Give the person you're committed to at least as much consideration.
3. Don't think all recreation things need to be done together. Have some things to do together and some things to do with others or alone.

Do's

1. Share the responsibility for planning recreational activities. Either discuss during the week what you're going to do over the weekend, or alternate planning the weekend's activities. If it's your turn to do the planning, try to think of something you'll *both* enjoy.
2. Even if you both have a very hectic schedule—working 60 hours at a job, taking care of children, etc.—make sure at least one weekend a month is spent playing or relaxing. If you forget how to have fun together, you'll be missing out on one of the major joys of being together.

A Closer Look at Common Conflict Areas

3. Allow time for quiet if you are an extravert or be willing to participate at times if you are an introvert. Once the initial resistance is gone, you may be surprised how much you enjoy the "other side."

Examples of How Your Viewpoint
Can Lead to Relationship Conflict

ISJs may say:	If you take a long time to do something, you're slow and compulsive; if I take a long time, I'm thorough.
EJs may say:	When you go ahead and do something without checking, you're testing my limits; when I go ahead and do something on my own, I'm showing initiative.
Ps may say:	If you don't follow through, you're lazy; when I don't follow through, I'm busy.
Js may say:	When you state your side strongly, you're being bull-headed; when I state my side strongly, I'm being firm.
SJs may say:	When you take on extra work at your job, you're ignoring the family's needs; when I do, I'm planning for the family's security.
Ns may say:	When you do something unexpected, you're inconsiderate; when I do something you weren't expecting, I'm original and creative.
ETJs may say:	If you get your chores done and have time to relax, you probably could have done a better job; if I finish my chores early, I'm an effective organizer and planner.

Worth thinking about?

Priority Factors in Conflicts

The next three areas of conflict that tend to be discussed in couple counseling sessions appear to be very related to type differences—particularly the judging-perceiving preference. These issues include Decision-Making, Responsibility, and Chores. The priorities each person establishes to respond to necessary the daily tasks of living together can set up conflicts. Expectations need to be discussed.

Decision-making

If you recall the descriptions of judging types and perceiving types from our first chapter, it may help you to understand why you may be experiencing difficulties when it's time for the two of you to arrive at a decision. If you have a clear preference for judging, you may feel uncomfortable while a decision is in process—whether that decision relates to where to go on vacation, which house to buy, or even which movie to go see. A perceiving partner, on the other hand, will be more comfortable while the decision is pending and less comfortable than you once the decision is made. Perceiving types find it hard to close off interesting options.

It is not unusual for us to have one individual state in a session, "I've made all our vacation plans for the last ten times—now I want you to do it!" If this individual is a judging type and their mate a perceiving type, we tend to discourage any alteration of this arrangement. Rather we try to help the judging type partner understand that the perceiving type has made their contribution by being willing to go along with pre-planning. It is comfortable and pleasant for judging types to have things decided. The perceiving type partner can contribute by providing many options within the structure when the event is actually occurring.

Judging types are happiest when plans are set well in advance, reservations made, tickets purchased and checked for accuracy; then they can relax! Perceiving types would often prefer to wait until close to the deadline to decide where they want to go—because, after all, they might hear of someplace new and exciting. If tickets are already purchased, they've lost the option of changing their minds.

If both of you are perceiving types, you may experience even more difficulty in this area. In a personal discussion with Isabel Myers, she shared with us the opinion that two perceiving types would encounter many problems when decisions would have to be made—that neither one enjoys the necessity of making a decision—and that whichever one wound up as the decision-maker would resent the other. Even though a judging type may not want the whole burden, they are at least getting their own needs met in the process; perceiving types often prefer more flexibility. Perhaps some things could be divided up by who dislikes the task least.

The danger for two judging types is that they might differ in the decision they arrive at, neither may have the flexibility to change, and a deadlock may occur. Resolution may come with some system for deciding who gets to decide this time and on what basis. Sometimes it could be based on the importance of the issue to each or simply that some things are in one partner's arena and some things are in the other's. Thinking-judging types especially can sound sure they are right, but are more willing to listen to a carefully thought out alternative than they appear.

Type differences can improve family decision-making, but in our experience also come up frequently as sources of conflict. To introverts, extraverts can seem to be impatient. To extraverts, introverts can seem to be slow. Sensing types may want to base decisions on short term goals and common sense. Intuitives will want to include the big picture and long term goals. Thinking types will want to decide with logic; feeling types will want to decide in favor of the people concerned. The judging-perceiving attitude may be the main one visible in decision-making, but the other functions and attitudes have their impact also. Every couple needs a process that works for them in arriving at a decision.

The recommended model for decision-making includes all four functions. Start with the facts, add the possibilities, process with logic and analysis, finish up with values:

$$S \rightarrow N \rightarrow T \rightarrow F$$

If you're experiencing difficulties in this area, we recommend:

Don'ts

1. Don't put the other down for being different from you, or devalue yourself for being different from your mate.
2. Don't let winning become more important than solving the problem.
3. Don't get outsiders to support your decision against your mate. Outsiders may bring it up later and that will be uncomfortable for you and them.

Do's

1. Examine your type and see how that may be affecting your interaction.
2. If you're both perceiving types, alternate responsibility for making the decisions ("I'll decide this week which movie or restaurant to go to; then you choose next week.")
3. If you have a dominant feeling function, even though you've made your decision as a feeling type, learn to present it in thinking form if your partner is a thinking type. Surely you can find some logical, objective rationale for the decision you've made.
4. If you're the partner with a preference for thinking, try to understand the effect of your decision on your partner's feelings. The actual statements are not as important as the recognition of the impact the decision may have and sensitivity to the possible results.

Resources

Lawrence, Gordon, *Zig-Zag Process for Problem-Solving*.
Myers, Katharine, *Decision Making and Type*.

Responsibility

A second area where type differences can be constructive or can cause conflict is in dividing family responsibilities. Responsibility may be more often picked up by judging types, but later resented if not shared by their partners. Sometimes, one partner doesn't pay attention to the imbalance. Sometimes, there is manipulation. For example, one partner in our practice said, "If I wait long enough I know my partner will do it." A good discussion and division of responsibilities based on talents and not gender is the best way to go. We think it is best to keep it fairly equal in terms of the time it takes to accomplish the task rather than the difficulty of the task—especially if the tasks are divided by who is good at what.

Everyone resists routine household maintenance. It is preferable to designate areas of responsibility that include some routine things and some creative things for each partner. A good discussion of the issues is often a tricky conversation and sometimes handled better in a counseling session where there is a "witness" to the agreement. Alternatively, a short term "contract" could be made subject to revisions, periodically.

Few people like to come home to an empty house. One ISJ woman seen in counseling had actually filed for divorce because her husband an ENP rarely showed up for dinner on time. ISFJs naturally expect people to be on time. He wouldn't be just twenty minutes late—often he'd be two or three hours late. Greg really loved Chris, considered himself a good husband, and genuinely could not understand why she would consider divorcing him. "I'm not out with other women", he would say, "and "I'm not gambling, or doing other things I know she would be justified in objecting to. It's just that after work a few of us guys talk over our accounts over a couple of beers and I hate to keep watching the clock."

With Greg and Chris, we decided to try something to address this difference in relating to time. We got him a wallet with "Call Chris" engraved in large letters. Whenever he would open it to pay a bar bill, he had an instant reminder in front of him. Chris also agreed that if he called, she would *not* ask him to come home. It was the lack of clarity rather than his presence that was of primary importance to her. She also agreed that if he were more than fifteen minutes late, she would eat with the children. He agreed that if she had already eaten, he would fix his own dinner (mostly warming leftovers) when he got home.

This does not appear to be an ideal solution, but it has worked for Chris and Greg. Their children are old enough so that if she knows he's going to be late, then she has options. She can visit a neighbor, go to a movie, or pick up a book rather than build up tension or anxiety waiting for his car to pull into the garage.

If you make enough money, it may be worth hiring someone to do the things you don't want to do, such as taxes. If you don't, it is better to divide up the responsibilities in some way you can both agree on. We suggest dividing by the time it takes to take care of that responsibility, i.e., if it takes 6 hours to do the income tax, do you share it or contribute in another area? If it takes two hours a day to prepare food, shop, and clean up, is that a shared responsibility or what is the tradeoff?

Type differences about time can cause a lot of minor annoyances that can lead to major blowups. "You're always late." "You always have to get there early." This usually centers on the judging-perceiving preferences. Judging types want an orderly world and things to run smoothly and on time. Perceiving types see time constraints as limiting their freedom and are uncomfortable and sometimes resistant. If both are in a partnership each needs to give a little so one partner is not uncomfortable more of the time. Judging types need not take perceiving types literally when they say "I'll be there by 8:00 p.m." If your experience is they tend to run an hour late, don't start counting until 9:00 p.m. Otherwise the perceiving type will not feel welcome when they do arrive and possibly stay out longer next time.

Perceiving types need to realize that judging types are not trying to control (in most instances)—just wanting the information so they can make their own plans. The problem is a perceiving type's agenda is flexible and a judging type's agenda is fairly fixed. Judging types can sometimes interpret that perceiving types are "lying" to them if they do something different than they intended or said they were going to do. Perceiving types need to avoid making statements that judging types can take literally. They need to build into the relationship the reality that they need a certain amount of room to move around and still be trusted. The trouble often is that since judging types prioritize early and their partners are their first priority, they more or less expect the same from their partners, not realizing that priorities can shift for perceiving types and are not so predictable.

Other type differences are also relevant to responsibility. Sensing types prefer tangible tasks and intuitives prefer abstract ones. Thinking types prefer logical tasks and feeling types prefer promoting harmonious interactions while working. Extraverts want someone with them while they're being responsible. Introverts would often prefer carrying out the responsibility by themselves.

It can be an act of love to fulfill the other person's needs if it does not diminish you in some way. If you're on time because you know I get upset when you're late, or you don't fuss at me when I get home because you know I need a little flexibility, our relationship can be enhanced. Changing for either type is harder than it looks. That's why in couples counseling, we look for something equally difficult for both partners. Both people need to take responsibility for the relationship.

If you're experiencing difficulty in this area, we recommend:

Don'ts

1. Don't start judging your partner without talking to them.
2. Don't rebel without understanding or telling your partner what it is that bothers you.
3. Don't always put your own agenda first; sometimes nurturing a relationship requires negotiation. Be open to discussion.

Do's

1. Try to be at least as courteous and attentive to your partner as you would to a client, customer, or co-worker.
2. Try to remember that your partner's behavior is a reflection of their type and not an indication of how much they love you.
3. Aim for a balance between the need for structure and the need for freedom. Allow time for fun as well as for getting the work done.

Chores

A third area of possible conflict in a relationship is chores. A clear and equal division of labor by the one most willing and able to accomplish the chore both by personality type and time available may help alleviate some of these difficulties.

There is a relationship, of course, between this category and the previous one of Responsibility. Chores are often repetitive but necessary. There appear to be some differences related to type. In both our counseling sessions and in our research, we find that extraverted women with introverted men are especially dissatisfied with the performance of chores—and so are the men. There appear to be several factors operating: introverted men are more likely to use up a lot of outgoing energy at work, especially if their occupation calls for considerable interaction, and want to be less active at home. Extraverted women are more likely to be involved in outside activities and have less time at home for performance of chores. Extraverts are also more likely to voice their complaints and demands. Complaints and demands rarely help an introvert get moving.

If both of you are intuitives, neither one of you is likely to derive any satisfaction from the performance of routine chores. If both of you are intuitives, it's especially important to share your thoughts and feelings about your expectations as to who will do what and to try to arrive at some equitable resolution.

Sensing types notice what needs to be done and can even be comfortable doing repetitive tasks in the interest of having things look nice and function well. Intuitives may not notice what needs to be done, but may like the results of a completed chore if they can "just do it" and not process it or resist it too long. It is probably good for type development to stretch ourselves to take care of the less interesting, but necessary tasks. The energy sometimes spent in disagreeing about whose task it is, could then be spent on "just doing it."

Making bridges between "to do" items in different roles may help facilitate the accomplishment of two or more items. For example, if exercise, picking up groceries, and spending more time with one's son can be combined into taking the son swimming and stopping for groceries on the way home, all these things will be accomplished, plus the potential for more enjoyment and companionship is present.

Being similar on the judging-perceiving preference seems easier here than being different. If you both agree on getting chores done according to schedule *or* if you both agree to be relaxed and spontaneous about the completion of chores, things run more smoothly. However, if getting things done on schedule is important to one of you and the other figures, "What's the big deal about when the dishes get done?" you may have to work out some trade-offs to achieve a fair division of labor.

If you are experiencing difficulty in this area, we recommend:

Don'ts

1. Don't get caught in the trap of thinking "If my partner loved me, of course I'd have a clean shirt to wear". Dislike for laundry has nothing to do with love. Another example might be "If my partner cared about me, my car would be fixed." Your partner may not be mechanically skilled.
2. Don't get caught in traps of "these are women's chores, those are men's." Do those chores that you truly prefer. If she loves to mow the lawn and he loves to cook, then that's how chores should be designated.
3. Don't let control or power issues make big deals out of little chores.

Do's

1. Make detailed lists, one of chores that have to be done on a daily basis, one of chores that need to be done on a weekly basis, and one of chores that need to be done only once or twice a year. Then on each list, each of you select the chores you enjoy doing—or mind doing the least—and initial those. Having signed up to accept this responsibility, you'll be less likely to argue later that you can't remember this agreement was made. If you can't agree on who's to do the others, put them in a hat and draw lots. Fair?
2. If you both work—and even if you don't but can afford it—hire household help to do the things you hate the most. One couple we saw, both professionals earning very decent salaries, almost broke up because she hated ironing his shirts, and he felt resentful every time he had to iron a shirt because they were all still sitting in the laundry basket. Implicit expectations can lead to problems. Be clear about what you want or need and check out those wants and needs with your partner.

Extraverted Thinking Types (ESTJ, ENTJ)	Will strategize. If that doesn't work, they may speed up their verbalization, overpower with the tone of their voice, and finally use explosions of anger to win their point. The competition is fierce, even when it gets rough.
Introverted Thinking Types (ISTP, INTP)	Will get so theoretical and abstract that you'll get lost following the maze they've constructed. You may finally give up just to get your mind "unboggled." If you understand, you must agree.
Extraverted Feeling Types (ESFJ, ENFJ)	May become very emotional, cry, and get angry. However, they do prefer harmony and want so much to be loved that their hearts aren't really in the fight. They'll concede fairly quickly if they can find a reason for conceding. Love is better than logic.
Introverted Feeling Types (ISFP, INFP)	Are likely to withdraw very quickly (either emotionally or physically) from any battle unless their primary values are at risk. If you think your introverted feeling type partner is a pushover, you're in for a surprise. There can be no compromise; ideals are ideals.

continued

A Closer Look at Common Conflict Areas

Extraverted Sensing Types (ESTP, ESFP)	Will enjoy the excitement of the fight, but their ability to see another's point of view and to be tolerant of it will finally help them to use all the available information to effect a compromise. The solution is more interesting than the fight.
Introverted Sensing Types (ISTJ, ISFJ)	Will know all the facts, all the rules and regulations that may pertain to the situation, and quote them.
Extraverted Intuitive Types (ENTP, ENFP)	Will take the wind out of your sails by seeming to agree with you—and suddenly, you'll find you're doing exactly what they wanted you to do in the first place. Off-balancing, but interesting.
Introverted Intuitive Types (INTJ, INFJ)	Will just out-stubborn you. If you think you can win a fight with an introverted intuitive type by shouting, manipulating, or coercing, you'll find that none of these tactics will work. They will quietly, but persistently, hold on to their own point of view and you'll find you've just wasted all your energy. You need to resolve it at a *deeper* level.

Other People as a Factor in Conflicts

The last set of problems seem to occur as a result of interactions with other people: Children, In-laws, and Friends. Positions taken, opinions expressed, support given or withheld, and possible judgments made by others are all examples of things that can influence a couple's interactions.

Children

Children can form the focus of a relationship. Couples can disagree about how to handle the children and avoid their own relationship. Children can play parents off against each other.

Children's types may become obvious early in life. Different types of children thrive under different styles of parenting. There are resources which can help bring perspective to your own style.

Differences and/or similarities on the MBTI do, of course, have an effect on the problems that arise in raising children. One issue that is often discussed in counseling sessions occurs when thinking types are partnered with feeling types. Since this tends to be a very common combination, many of you may be dealing with a similar problem. Feeling type parents are apt to opt for harmony and good feelings in the home, and in relationships with their children. If a thinking type parent appears critical or demanding of performance and the children get hurt or upset, the feeling type parent is likely to be upset also.

Values as to how children are to be raised and disciplined may differ greatly, and differences in values are not easy to negotiate. Actually, parents can provide a balance for each other's perceptions if they do not oppose each other's positions too exclusively. Both some support and some requirements for performance are necessary for children. Each parent can value the other's contribution if they don't become too locked into their own perceptions.

Extraverted parents tend to encourage activity and interaction. Introverted parents find it easier to let children be alone to read or enjoy quiet times. Children can learn good skills from each.

Intuitive parents can have more problems with some of the confining routines involved in parenting. This does not in any sense mean that intuitive parents love their children less than sensing parents, only that their reactions to routine are different. Intuitive parents may teach imaginative games.

Sensing parents may prefer taking care of day to day needs, providing comfort and security.

It is easier for thinking types to be firm. It is easier for feeling types to be demonstratively loving. Children need both.

Judging types are better at providing structure which children need. Perceiving types find it easier to provide the space to explore which children also need. Your styles can complement each other.

When you encounter difficult challenges with children, we recommend:

Don'ts

1. Don't repeat the same parenting style you received unless you think it was a very good one. It is a very easy thing to just follow unconsciously in an old pattern even if it is not functional. Try to stay aware and make good choices in your parenting.
2. Don't think of discipline as punishment. If the children don't learn from you, they will learn later from the world—and it can be a much harder teacher. Think of discipline as part of their education until they can learn to discipline themselves. A "discipline" is really something that can be learned and is related to education and knowledge.
3. Don't let the children be a divisive force, especially if one child is your type and another one is your partner's type. Don't let it be the intuitive-feeling types against the sensing-thinking types any more than men against women or vice versa.
4. Don't, no matter how much you love them, let your children become the ruling passion in your life. Even if you can't afford it, find a way to get away at times with your partner and renew your relationship. The children will be gone someday, and you won't want to discover that there's nothing left between you.
5. Don't leave the raising of the children totally in your partner's hands, no matter how capable they are. Children need both parents, not just financial support. Introverted parents need to save some energy for what can be an exciting and rewarding adventure in getting to know who they are and who you are. And a little child may lead you toward wholeness!

Do's

1. Model being a good human being with many possible behaviors, so your children can learn by example from you and/or your partner.

2. If your feeling function is your dominant function, and your partner *and* children are thinking types, leave the room or the house when they begin to argue or send barbs back and forth. They really do enjoy the dueling and *you* will be the only one who gets hurt if you stay there. Don't attempt to be a peacemaker between individuals who are enjoying the war.

3. If there are many basic differences between you, sometimes taking courses such as Parent Effectiveness Training or Tough Love can help you to see the value in what your mate has to offer, while at the same time helping to make you a team.

4. Teach love and respect by the way you treat the children and each other.

5. Both fathers and mothers can help children of both sexes with their identity by understanding and appreciating differences. Keep communication lines open to gain a better understanding of the children as well as each other.

Resources

Murphy, Elizabeth, *The Developing Child: Using Jungian Type to Understand Children.*

Wickes, Frances, *The Inner World of Childhood.*

In-laws

In Hawaii, there are many extended families. Among Asians, especially, family is an important priority which affects the in-law situation. Even a "small" wedding here is 200 people or more when all family members and "calabash" aunties and uncles are included. Since Hawaii is relatively small geographically, it is difficult to not be affected by family members for those who are second, third, or fourth generation local residents.

Other people who can deeply affect a relationship definitely include in-laws. Most family members rely on your presentation of your partner in forming their conclusions and responses about how they will relate to that person. Some members may be angry if time, attention, or money they have been receiving become less as a result of your new relationship. Others may be happy if they perceive you are generally happy with your partner. Some may give too much advice; some may not want to be involved. The responses can be as varied as the individuals concerned.

Through it all though, the in-laws will look to you for some clues about how to respond to your partner. Depending on the types involved some difficulties can be bridged easier than others. Judging types tend to form a conclusion about people and work off that hypothesis unless presented with other explicit contradictory data. A positive evaluation is not easily dislodged—but neither is a negative one. Perceiving types can seem more tolerant, often because they have not seen it necessary for them to form any conclusions about the new family member. They are comfortable staying in process.

Extraverted feeling and introverted sensing types (both judging types) are more likely to meet in-laws' expectations and to want to meet them. Thinking types are often less bothered by expectations as long as they are treated with respect.

Introverts may be reluctant participants in large family gatherings of their in-laws. Their partners may need to be willing to go alone sometimes to these functions if they occur often.

Extraverts will welcome social get-togethers and want to have and attend a variety of such functions. Introvert partners need to be willing to participate in the important ones.

Sensing types may need to be patient with in-laws that seem to be dreamers and lack "common sense." Intuitive types may need to be patient with in-laws who seem rigid and reality bound.

Feeling types may need to protect themselves in some family situations in which their values may get "offended" and they may interpret things negatively. Thinking types need to stay away from religion, politics, and other "loaded" topics especially if they have a need to be "right."

Perceiving types may need to be more willing to stay longer than they would like at family dinners. Judging types may need to loosen up if their assessment of the situation makes them negative.

What is expected in the way of interaction with in-laws is dependent not only on ethnic background and culture, but also on the relationship between son or daughter and parents. If you're aware that your partner has a close and warm relationship with their parents, that partner will want you to be close to them also—and to share in family dinners, picnics, etc. If your partner is angry and rebelling against their parents, there will be less interaction with the family, but also some of the anger may spill off on you. If your partner is close and very involved with family, you may wind up feeling that the family comes first. If your partner is distant and detached with family, is that partner capable or willing to have an intimate relationship with you?

If there are problems in this area, we recommend:

Don'ts

1. Don't put your partner into the position of having to choose sides between you and their parents.
2. Don't go into business with, borrow money from, or live with in-laws if you can avoid it.
3. Don't let yourself get away with showing your negative side if you choose to attend in-law functions. Go when you know you can take part willingly.
4. Don't expect your partner to stay all day with the in-laws unless that is comfortable for your partner.

Do's

1. Try to put some physical distance between your home and your parents home. Minimize the expectations that your relationship values will correspond with those of parents on either side.
2. Help your partner understand the family system; introduce them in ways that facilitate acceptance of one another.
2. If it's *your* parents, you take on the task of turning down an invitation, reminding them of how you want the children disciplined, etc. Don't let parents come between you and your partner any more than you would allow children to do so.
3. The social ease of the extravert, the depth of the introvert, the common sense of the sensing type, the creativity of the intuitive type, the flexibility of the perceiving type, and the commitment of the judging type can each help to make in-law relations better. Thinking types can contribute their wit and feeling types can contribute harmony and cooperation.

Friends

Friends are the third group or people who may influence relationships. Friends can impact a relationship in many ways. They often tend to be supportive rather than objective. Referring to the fact that opposite types often marry and friends tend to be similar types, Joe Wheelwright, a Jungian therapist in San Francisco, once said (paraphrased) "So you can wind up being married to someone you wouldn't even have for a friend." He was noting how challenging a marital relationship can be as well as pointing out that something less conscious is occurring when choosing a partner that is not occurring when choosing a friend. We believe at least some people have now developed to a point where our partners can also be our friends although it may take some work.

It does tend to be true that we choose friends who are more similar to ourselves, and then we don't have to work as hard at relating. We recommend each partner have friends of their own and friends in common. Each needs to take care that the separate friendships do not detract from, but rather enhance, the primary relationship. This means choosing the time wisely to be with the separate friends and not slipping over into a romantic or sexual involvement with them.

Extraverts tend to have more friends they want to socialize with; introverts tend to have fewer and deeper friendships and enjoy sociability with smaller numbers.

Sensing types tend to look for an experience and activities along with their friendships and the conversation; intuitive types also often want experiences but the experiences can be metaphysical, not necessarily "reality" centered.

Thinking types like to verbally spar and may look for a sparring companion as a friend; feeling types may look for a friend with whom they experience harmony and good "vibrations" without sparring.

Perceiving types who like to keep their options open, may pick up with one friend for awhile, move onto another and then return to the first or a variety of others. Judging types are more likely to want to be with their "best friend" more of the time.

The extraverted qualities of being outgoing and socially at ease that attracted a more introverted partner in the first place may prove an irritant once they are living together. Women, in general, extravert or introvert, tend to want to have close friendships with other women, and this, too, can be an irritant to males who believe they are being discussed and criticized with "strangers." Women may also worry and wonder about how men talk about them or women in general, when the men get together.

According to the Hite report (1987), women turn to female friends because they often have some difficulty in sharing emotional intimacy with their male partners. In our experience, thinking type males, especially men who also prefer introversion, often experience powerful emotions of anger, tenderness, or sadness that they do not express for fear of being vulnerable or out of control. We have also seen hundreds of men learn to appreciate and participate in emotional intimacy, although it does seem to come more easily for feeling males than for thinking males. Men can certainly share feelings and emotions to the degree that women may truly feel their male partner is their "best friend," even though he may not communicate to the same extent and/or depth as the other women in her life.

In addition, it is important for individuals to respect the needs their partner may have for some solitary pursuits, as well as needs for some shared activities with friends for both partners.

If you are experiencing difficulty in this area, we recommend:

Don'ts

1. Don't be critical of your partner's friends so that your partner is driven to defend them. If you think the friend is getting more attention than you are, ask for what you need from your partner. Discriminate whether you really don't like the person or whether you're feeling left out.
2. Don't sulk or make scenes at parties. If you really don't want to be there, you have options. Don't go, find a way to leave early (take two cars, if this is likely to happen), or "put on a happy face." You can help create a pleasant experience for the individual you loved enough to live with or marry. You may even find you enjoy the party yourself.

Do's

1. Work out a time with each other for mutual social engagements, engagements in which you participate with your own friends, and time to be alone with each other. The balance you develop will of course depend on your own types (especially the extravert-introvert and thinking-feeling preferences) and your own work patterns.
2. If one of you is a judging type and the other a perceiving type, take advantage of this difference. Let the judging type schedule activities with friends; let the perceiving type create spontaneous, fun happenings with friends.
3. If you're an introvert, let your extraverted friends help pull you out into the world and its activities.
4. If you're an extravert, let your introverted friends teach you how to meditate or stop the action for awhile and be at peace.

This is, of course, by no means an exhaustive list of problems that couples bring into therapy to resolve. But an understanding of type, along with mutual respect and a sense of humor, can help couples work out differences.

Tips for Couples

1. Descriptions of type are often more accurate for 20 to 30 year olds than those who are older or much younger because of the developmental process of life.
2. The individuation process encourages developing your other functions and attitudes, and the opposites tend to emerge as we grow older.
3. In the best relationships, your partner encourages and contributes to your growth as a person and your growth in your chosen occupation.
4. The best way to have some control of your unconscious (less-preferred) side is to acknowledge it and make friends with it.
5. Women's masculine side and men's feminine side need acceptance by each other and by themselves.

Resources

Association for Psychological Type
9140 Ward Parkway
Kansas City, Missouri 64114
(816) 444-3500

Center for Applications of Psychological Type
2815 NW 13th Street, Suite 401
Gainesville, Florida 32609
(352) 375-0160

Consulting Psychologists Press
3803 East Bayshore Road
Palo Alto, California 94303
(415) 969-8901

Afterword

Reflections from Ruth. . .

Over the years of closely observing the relationships of clients, family, peers, and friends, I have come to believe that there are just a very few basic ingredients required if a relationship is to be mutually satisfying and growth producing.

I believe it is important for both partners to possess a healthy sense of self-esteem. Without this, one is too susceptible to issues of control, manipulation, and possible rejection.

Another necessary ingredient is mutual respect. If two individuals respect each other they will want to hear what the other has to offer, whether it is in the area of business, thoughts, feelings, or the raising of children regardless of the differences or similarities between them.

These two ingredients are important from the beginning of the relationship, but even if they are missing they can be developed during the course of the relationship.

The third ingredient is rarely developed before the basic business of the relationship has been resolved. That business includes issues such as who pays the bills, how to discipline the children, and how much of a social life to lead. These may now be past history, and life can begin to seem meaningless. This malaise undoubtedly contributes to the mid-life crisis experienced by so many individuals.

The soul cannot be filled by a divorce, by moving to a South Seas island, or by a change in career. What is soul satisfying is to share with a mate at a more spiritual level. This may include (but not necessarily) a deeper commitment to a church or established institution, writing a book together, sharing a love of poetry, gardening, or any area in which both can be creative and share that creativity with each other.

Reflections from Jane...

I am convinced that maintaining an important relationship is the major challenge and reward of life. I am also convinced that the way to do this is to develop your own soul to the maximum extent possible given the limitations at hand. In writing this book, we made a sincere effort to speak as one voice, but to even approximate the goal required a lot of checking, re-writing, thought, and negotiating.

Watching the couples skating as pairs in the Olympics, I was struck with the metaphor for a relationship such skaters were demonstrating. Male and female, different in gender, but partners flowing in unison. A clearly orches-trated piece—did they manage it by themselves or have help? Looking at what makes for championship couple skating, certain facts seemed to emerge about the skaters—

> They care
> They care about themselves and each other
> They are committed to themselves and each other
> They share a common goal
> Self-discipline is necessary to achieve results
> They work hard, but the result is worth the effort
> They are not the same, but each is equally important
> Their steps are different, but they flow together
> If one stumbles, it affects the other deeply
> They can only accomplish their goal through a harmonious interaction...

This is only a small beginning—perhaps the reader can add his or her own interpretations of the metaphor to his or her own life and relationship.

Jung's psychology and the Myers-Briggs Type Indicator are about making the world a better place and helping resolve some of the pain through under-standing and healing. Relationships are in need of both. In Jane's years of working with people, first as a teacher and then as a therapist, what stands out is the transformation that occurs when a spiritual resolution or soul-level transformation takes place. It is truly experienced from inside and out as a miracle.

Sacred Places Inside

We have been pleased to see the new emphasis on soul in writings as we are sure that it is the only real place of healing. Many times even physical ailments can only get well if body and spirit work together. We all know people who have willed themselves to die and been able to bring it about. If we but turn that power on life, what miracles may we accomplish! This is not accomplished by being some kind of "pussy-cat" as one of our friends is wont to say of people who don't stand up for themselves and to life, but by bringing the "beauty" and the "beast" together within to own the power of each.

In Memoriam
Ruth April Sherman
September 3, 1921–April 3, 1996.

Bibliography

Campbell. J. (ed.), *The Portable Jung*, Penguin Books, New York, New York, 1971.

Comfort, A., *The Joy of Sex*, Crown Publishing, New York, New York, 1987.

Elston, L., *Square Pegs and Round Holes: How to Match the Personality to the Job*, First Step Enterprises, San Diego, California, 1984.

Grant, W. H., Thompson, M., & Clarke, T. E., *From Image to Likeness: A Jungian Path in the Gospel Journey* Paulist Press. Ramsey, New Jersey, 1983.

Hill, G. S., *Masculine and Feminine: The Natural Flow of Opposites in the Psyche*, Shambhala Press, Boston, Massachusetts, 1992.

Hirsh, S. K., & Kummerow, J. M., *LIFETypes*. Warner Books, New York, 1989.

Isachsen, O., & Berens, L. V., *Working Together* (2nd ed.). Neworld Management Press, Coronado, California, 1991.

Jung, C. G., *Modern Man in Search of a Soul*, translated by W.S. Dell and C.F. Baynes; Harcourt Brace, New York, 1933.

Jung, C. G., *Psychological Types*, Princeton University Press, Princeton, New Jersey, 1971.

Jung, C. G., *Two Essays on Analytical Psychology*, translated by R.F.C. Hull, The World Publishing Co., New York, 1953.

Jung, E., *Animus and Anima*, Spring Publications, Switzerland, 1957.

Keirsey, D. and Bates, M., *Please Understand Me*, Prometheus Nemesis Books, Del Mar, California, 1978.

Kinsey, A. C., Pomeroy, W. B., and Marten, C. E., *Sexual Behavior in the Human Male*, W.B. Saunders, Philadelphia, 1948.

Kinsey, A. C., Pomeroy, W. B., Marten, C. E. and Gibhard, P. H., *Sexual Behavior in the Human Female*, W.B. Saunders, Philadelphia, 1953.

Kroeger, O. and Thuesen, J. M., *Type Talk*, Delacourte Press, New York, 1988.

Kroeger, O., & Thuesen, J. M., *16 ways to Love Your Lover: Understanding the 16 Personality Types So You Can Create a Love That Lasts Forever*, Delacorte Press, New York, 1994.

Kummerow, J. M., *Talking in Type* [Training handout]. Center for Applications of Psychological Type, Gainesville, Florida, 1985.

Kummerow, J. M., *Verifying Your Type Preferences* [Training handout], Center for Applications of Psychological Type Gainesville, Florida, 1986.

Larken, C., *Headlines of My Life*, Human Perspectives, Del Mar, California, 1989.

Lawrence, G. D., *People Types and Tiger Stripes*, Center for Applications of Psychological Type, Inc., Gainesville, Florida, 1979.

Lawrence, G. D., *Communications Patterns* [Training handout], Center for Applications of Psychological Type, Gainesville, Florida, 1985.

Lawrence, G. D., *The Zig-Zag Process for Problem Solving* [Training handout], Center for Applications of Psychological Type, Gainesville, Florida, 1988.

Masters, W. H. and Johnson, V. E., *Human Sexual Inadequacy*, Little Brown, Boston, 1970.

Meier, C. A., *Personality: The Individuation Process in the Light of C. G. Jung's Typology*, Daimon, Einsiedeln, Switzerland, 1971.

Murphy, E., *The Developing Child: Using Jungian Type to Understand Children*, Consulting Psychologists Press, Palo Alto, California, 1992.

Myers, I. B., *Manual: The Myers-Briggs Type Indicator*, Educational Testing Service, Princeton, New Jersey, 1962.

Myers, I. B., *Introduction to Type*, Isabel Briggs Myers, Swarthmore, Pennsylvania, 1970.

Myers, I. B., & McCaulley, M. H. *Manual: A Guide to the Development and Use of the Myers-Briggs Type Indicator*, Consulting Psychologists Press, Palo Alto, California, 1985.

Myers, I. B. and Myers, P. B., *Gifts Differing*, Consulting Psychologists Press, Palo Alto, California, 1980.

Myers, K. D., *Decision Making and Type* [Training handout], Center for Applications of Psychological Type, Gainesville, Florida, 1985.

Page, E. C., *Looking at Type* (2nd ed.). Center for Applications of Psychological Type, Gainesville, Florida, 1992.

Quenk, N. L., *Beside Ourselves: Our Hidden Personality in Everday Life* Davies-Black Publishing, Palo Alto, California, 1993.

Sherman, R., *Psychological Typology and Satisfaction in Intimate Relationships*, Unpublished Doctoral Dissertation, Saybrook Institute, 1981.

Sherman, R.G., *Typology and Problems in Intimate Relationships*, Research in Psychological Type, 4, 4-23, 1981.

Smith, J. C., *Psychoanalytic Roots of the Patriarchy: The Neurotic Roots of Social Order*, New York University Press, New York, 1990.

Von Franz, M. L. and Hillman, J., *Lectures on Jung's Typology*, Spring Publications, New York, 1971.

Wheelwright, J., *Psychological Types*, C.G. Jung Institute of San Francisco Publication.

Wickes, F. G., *The Inner World of Childhood*, New American Library, New York, 1966.

Wyse, L., *Love Poems for the Very Married*, Garret Press, Colorado Springs, Colorado, 1967.

Bibliography

Literature for Further Reading

Bernard, J. S., *The Future of Marriage*, World Publishing Co., New York, 1972.

Bradway, K., Jung's Psychological Types, *Journal of Analytical Psychology*, Tamstock Publishing, London, 9, 129-135, 1964.

Jung, C. G., *Memories, Dreams, Reflections*, ed. Amelia Jaffe, Pantheon Books, New York, 1963.

Jung, C. G., *Modern Man in Search of a Soul*, translated by W. S. Dell and C. F. Baynes; Harcourt Brace, New York, 1933.

Jung, C. G., *Two Essays on Analytical Psychology*, translated by R. F. C. Hull, The World Publishing Co., New York, 1953.

Jung, C. G., *The Collected Works of C.G. Jung*, Princeton University Press, Princeton, New Jersey, 1971. (Bollingen Series XX)

Keirsey, D., *Portraits of Temperament*, Prometheus Nemesis Book Co., Del Mar, California, 1987.

Keyserling, C. H., *The Book of Marriage*, Harcourt Brace, New York, 1926.

Rogers, C. R., *Becoming Partners*, Delacourte Press, New York, 1972.

Von Franz, M.L., *The Way of the Dream*, Windron Films Ltd., Toronto, Canada, 1988.